WOMAN IN  WHOL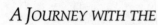

A JOURNEY WITH THE

REFLECTION, RELAXATION AND RESPONSE

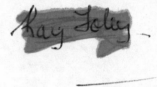

WOMAN IN SEARCH OF WHOLENESS

A JOURNEY WITH THE SAMARITAN WOMAN

REFLECTION, RELAXATION AND RESPONSE

ANNE ALCOCK

MERCIER PRESS

MERCIER PRESS
5 French Church Street, Cork
and
16 Hume Street, Dublin 2

Trade enquiries to COLUMBA MERCIER DISTRIBUTION,
55a Spruce Avenue, Stillorgan Industrial Park, Blackrock, Dublin

© Anne Alcock, 2002

1 85635 391 5

10 9 8 7 6 5 4 3 2 1

TO MOMMA-JAN HANLON – CALIFORNIA

ACKNOWLEDGMENTS
The illustration of Stephen Broadbent's sculpture, *The Water of Life*, from the cloister garden in Chester Cathedral is by kind permission of the Cathedral Chapter.

Scripture quotations marked *(TLB)* are taken from *The Living Bible*, copyright © 1971. Used by permission of Tyndale House Publishers, Inc., Wheaton, IL 60189 USA. All rights reserved.

'The Journey' by Mary Eleanore Rice, 'Images' by Betsy Phillips Fisher, 'The Middle-Time' by Lona Fowler, 'Divine Whisperings' by Edith Griswold Farey and 'A Gift' by Mary Eleanore Rice are all reprinted from *Images of Women in Transition*, by Janice Grana (Saint Mary's Press, Winona, MN, 1991). Used by permission of the publisher. All rights reserved.

'Desert Pathways' by Patricia Lennon and 'Potter's Hands' by Diarmuid Kerrisk are reprinted by permission of the authors.

Printed in Ireland by Colour Books Ltd.

CONTENTS

CONTENTS

FOREWORD

Why the Samaritan woman? I suppose, first of all, whether she is real, or a Scriptural metaphor, I simply like her. Dogged, dependable or just persistent, she keeps coming back to the well. I can relate to that. Secondly, having suggested her story as a reflection and prayer text to almost everyone who ever came on an individually-guided retreat, I've found that she makes deep connections with others too. Perhaps we see our own inner growth in her jerky, honest, personal process. Whatever it is, she seems like a friend. Her responses sound familiar. We can catch hold of them to bring us deeper into our own self-Self, self-God relationship. Her story localises familiar but specific themes, like finding our real name, looking at our hopes, experiencing conflict, opting out, identifying real desires, weighing costs, letting-go, and coming home to our own skin. Most of us know from experience that these bear re-visiting from time to time in quiet evaluation, when we have a few days off, as well as in longer periods of more focused discernment.

The content of each chapter is based on a small section of the story of the Samaritan woman, and each provides a loose framework for personal reflection, following the format of the 'Samaritan woman' retreat which first took place about fifteen years ago. Although often asked to do so, I always said I would never be able to put this together as a book, because 50 per cent of the dynamic happens outside the sessions, and of course details of content change as well. But the more I've listened to people, the more I realise that the basic story continues to provide new insights of personal growth. Therefore, aware that my words are merely surface-stirrings on the waters of a deeper well, I have finally attempted what I used to resist.

The collection of thoughts and stories, visualisations and

questions, hopefully opens up the vaster space between the printed words. This is your own depths. From there on, the well, the detail, and the mystery are yours.

Preface

She keeps coming back to a well. And what is the purpose of her coming and going? What is the quality? Is it always as it has been? Is it always what she expects? Does she even have any expectations? Who knows? And do we also always come back, again and again, like the Samaritan woman, with a question in our heart? Where am I coming from? Where am I going? Who knows? We can only begin where we are. With the setting.

At a significant junction on a much-travelled road, between the mountain of Curses and the mountain of Blessing (Mounts Ebal and Gerazim) is this well. Known as Bir Ya'qub, Jacob's well, it has supplied the link to life reaching back for generations, yet still supplies freely. As we approach it here, it stands at a crossroads, situated at the mid-point of a journey, between a leaving and an arriving. It is the place to pause, and take an overview.

Jesus is on his way home.

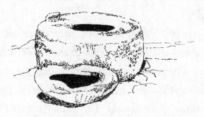

He had to go through Samaria on the way, and around noon, as he approached the village of Sychar, he came to Jacob's well, on the plot of ground Jacob gave to his son Joseph. Jesus was tired from the long walk in the hot sun and sat wearily beside the well.

Soon a Samaritan woman came to draw water and Jesus asked her for a drink. He was alone at the time, as his disciples had gone into the village to buy some food. The woman was surprised that a Jew would ask a 'despised Samaritan' for anything – usually they wouldn't even speak to them – and she remarked about this to Jesus.

He replied, 'if you only knew what a wonderful gift God has for you, and who I am, you would ask me for some living water.'

'But you don't have a rope or a bucket,' she said, 'and this is a very deep well. From where would you get this living water? And besides, are you greater than our ancestor Jacob? How can you offer better water than this, which he and his sons and cattle enjoyed?'

Jesus replied that people soon became thirsty again after drinking this water. 'But the water I give them,' he said, 'becomes a perpetual spring within them, watering them forever with eternal life.'

'Please sir,' the woman said, 'give me some of that water! Then I'll never be thirsty again, and won't have to make this long trip out here every day.'

'Go and get your husband,' Jesus told her.

'But I'm not married,' the woman replied.

'All too true!' Jesus said. 'For you have had five husbands, and you aren't even married to the man you're living with now.

'Sir,' the woman said, 'you must be a prophet. But tell me, why is it that you Jews insist that Jerusalem is the only place of worship, while we Samaritans claim it is here at Mount Gerazim, where our ancestors worshipped?'

Jesus replied, 'The time is coming when we will no longer be concerned about whether to worship the Father here or in Jerusalem. For it is not where we worship that counts, but how we worship. Is our worship spiritual and real? For God is Spirit, and we must have his help to worship as we should. The Father wants this kind of worship from us. But you Samaritans know so little about him, worshipping blindly, while we Jews know all about him, for salvation comes to the world through the Jews.'

The woman said, 'Well, at least I know that the Messiah will come – the one they call Christ – and when he does, he will explain everything to us.'

Then Jesus told her, 'I am the Messiah'.

Just then his disciples arrived. They were surprised to find him talking to a woman, but none of them asked him why, or what they had been discussing.

Then the woman left her water-pot beside the well and went back to the village and told everyone, 'Come and meet a man who told me everything I ever did! Can this be the Messiah?' So the people came streaming from the village to see him.

Meanwhile, the disciples were urging Jesus to eat. 'No,' he said, 'I have some food you don't know about.'

'Who brought it to him?' the disciples asked each other.

Then Jesus explained: 'My nourishment comes from doing the will of God who sent me, and from finishing his work.'

JOHN 4:4–34 (*TLB*)

APPROACHING WITH OPEN HANDS

(A fifteen-minute revitaliser, seven or eight minutes each hand – or longer, if you wish to linger with a suitably-diluted essential oil of your choice.)

Sitting down comfortably, hands relaxed in your lap or supported at waist level, begin by taking a deep, into-the-belly, breath. Lift your shoulders towards your ears, hold them there a moment, and then gently let them drop. This is not a 'heady' exercise, as you are simply pressing different areas of your hand in turn. You may be aware of different textures, bony, hard, soft, ticklish, and you may sense a little renewal of energy, especially as you come to the end, when you rub each finger and massage the wrists. Sometimes you also feel an echo in your

11

feet, as tingling, aliveness. I have introduced a couple of lines from Psalm 139 as you move to the second hand. This is like just dipping a hand into the water, as one way among many, to centre and focus as you sit down at the well. So settle in and begin by placing your right thumb into the centre of your left palm, and then let that thumb explore all over your left palm, for a minute or so. Just let your thumb roll and press – with a personally-comfortable pressure – the different contours of your palm. Relax your tummy. Now press the very centre of your palm, and if it feels natural, just breathe in and out like a sigh, letting the day's tensions release. From that centre, think of your hand as a fan-shaped shell, and let your thumb climb up the little pathways between the bones of the palm, like a small firm caterpillar on the surface of the skin, denting it slightly or firmly, up to the top of the hand, about six little steps, then lifting off the thumb and returning it to the fan's centre for the next upward trip. Relax your shoulders.

Now locate that 'v' of fleshy skin joining the base of the receiving thumb to the whole side of the palm, and massage all over, whatever way works for you, with the fingers as well as the thumb, of your giving hand. Slip your giving thumb very slightly upwards and right, until it is just under (not on) the palm-knuckle of the index (second) finger. Press and roll. Relax your tummy. Now come up to the fingerprint pad of the receiving thumb, roll and press, supporting the back of that thumb with the fingers of the giving hand. Move on to doing the same with each finger-tip in turn, second, third, fourth, fifth, and then return the giving thumb to the receiving palm, while rubbing the back of that hand in a circular movement, with the fingers of the giving hand.

Now swap hands, so the left thumb is now exploring the right palm. You may find the sensations and texture slightly different. Do we know our own hands? What does this hand hold? 'Oh Lord, you search me and you know me, you know my resting and my rising' (Psalm 139:1–2). No need to rush on, if you choose to stay; no need even to finish the sequence. Stop, as the Samaritan woman does, where you find the Lord. Or, as we move on, bringing your thumb to the centre of your receiving palm, and gently press, on an out-breath. 'Into your hands

…' Then once again locating that 'v' of fleshy skin, that joins thumb to side of hand, just use the fingers and thumb of your new giving hand to roll and massage this. Relax your shoulders. Move your left thumb very slightly up and to the left, until it is just below, not on, the palm-knuckle of the index (second) finger. Press, and roll. Relax, breathe out and say your name to yourself, even as a whisper or out loud. 'I'm here.' Close your eyes for a moment, and be here. When you're ready, caterpillar-walk your giving thumb upwards between the bones of your palm. Like little pathways. 'Lord, make me know your ways. Lord, teach me your paths. – Show me my path' (Psalm 25:4). Now come up to the pad of the receiving thumb, supporting it with the fingers of the giving hand, and rolling and pressing the pad. Relax your shoulders. The point relates to the head area – 'You understand my thoughts from afar.' Now press the tips of each of the second, third, fourth and fifth fingers in turn, and breathe, receiving the breath – cool air breathed in, warm air breathed out. Return your left thumb to the centre of your right palm, and massage the back of your hand with the fingers of your left hand, in a circular movement. Bring both hands together for an all-over rub, as if washing them. Gently pull down the length of each finger of both hands (not cracking the knuckles!) and feel the waking-up. Circle your fingers around each wrist in turn and turn it rapidly within the circle. Then, rub your hands vigorously together for a moment or two, and, then let them settle naturally into the gesture which best expresses the sense of yourself and how you are at this time. Pray out of this.

1
MID-DAY PAUSE

THE JOURNEY

where are you going i asked
to places i have never been
was the answer
what do you plan to do i asked
my purpose will be evident at journey's end
who has planned your itinerary i asked
its plan will be revealed at times most unlikely
why would you consent to such a vague plan i said
i accepted the challenge
when i accepted life was the answer

MARY ELEANORE RICE

He had to go through Samaria on the way, and around noon, as he
approached the village of Sychar, he came to Jacob's well, on the plot of
ground Jacob gave to his son Joseph. Jesus was tired from the long walk
in the hot sun and sat wearily beside the well.

The journey to anywhere begins from where we are and how we
are. Or as someone once said, 'Where we are with where we are
is more important than where we are'. So we might start by re-
reading the short text above, and seeing which words we
connect with most. 'I never got beyond the part where it says
Jesus is tired,' said Brenda, 'it made me realise that I was tired
too.' She arrived for a reflection-day, with a full personal agenda,
and several books – and then just came to a halt. Does this sound
familiar? Would you find that, like Brenda, you connect with the
words 'was tired', 'sat wearily', or 'had to go through'? I cer-
tainly do, and other comments I have heard are 'My life seems
to be an ever-widening circle. I'm running fast, but going nowhere. If I stopped running I'd fall apart' and 'I have been pres-

14

surising myself on the work-front, and pushing everything else to the edge.' Of course what really gets pushed to the edge is ourselves.

If this were the first session of the original Samaritan woman prayer-and-process workshop, I would probably begin by turning our attention to how we are sitting. Do we sit, or do we 'perch' – leaning forward on the edge of the chair, reaching into tomorrow? If yes, let's slow down – even our reading of this book.

We might do an all-over body-scan, using the 'how am I?' question again, as we move our attention from section to section in as much detail, or not, as time allows, letting our body itself answer, because it is better at answering than our mind, which prefers to deny what doesn't fit our schedule or our image. So if you start with your feet and work slowly upwards to your head, and along your arms, are your muscles relaxed, or is there any part that feels tight and could use a gentle stretch? If you lift your shoulders up towards your ears, hold them there a moment or two, until you are aware of the feeling of warmth and stretch, and then gently let them go, can you sense how much further they have dropped? And the jaw. If you allow your back teeth to open ever so slightly, and soften your lips and your eyes, can you feel any difference? And finally, in this check-in, we might notice the breath – that key to calm – as it comes and goes with the ease of a sleeping baby, rather than in short, shallow puffs. From where do you usually breathe? Top of chest, around the sternum, as far down as the ribs and intercostal muscles, or deeply, as a full-belly breath?

Interestingly, many of us are still trying to re-learn how to breathe naturally, after half-a-lifetime, of being taught to hold our breath in when we take a breath, and of course, 'pull in your tummy!' But an in-breath involves taking-in air, so our tummy actually expands as it does so, allowing maximum filling, and then a real emptying out-breath. We can't force breathing, but we can be aware when we inhibit it. There is a deep breathing

15

exercise at the end of this reflection.

Finally, in this brief 'how are you?' before meeting the Samaritan woman, and engaging with the rest of the story, if you were asked, as on the workshop, to express how you are today, through colour, form or line, what would emerge? I've seen smooth spirals, circles and waves, aquamarine, and pastel. Zig-zags, jagged lines, strong colours, plus black, and scrunched paper with deep-scored lines. What else?

If you are wondering what this all has to do with a text of Scripture, I suppose it is that the Scripture story passes us back to our own story, and this particular section of text seems to offer such a perfect introduction to awareness of the wholeness of who we are, body, mind and spirit.

In it, Jesus is described as tired. (Not for the first time; we have seen him resting on a boat-journey as told in Matt. 8:24, Mark 4:38, Luke 8:23.) Now he is on land, on the fast route home through Samaria, taking time out from hassle and misunderstanding. About halfway along, his body signals that it is weary, and that it is time to slow down. He responds by acknowledging this, and taking a rest. Would we? Well of course, his tiredness did come from physical effort, and anyway, he was a carpenter. Is this significant? Apparently. 'Labourers, craftsmen and people who use their muscles in their work, are more in touch with their rest-cycles than are office-workers, professional people, housewives, house-husbands, and teachers ...(yet) *mental and emotional efforts take an equal amount of energy as, say, a carpenter building a house. The only difference is that different parts of the body are doing the work.*[1] Of course fatigue signals arising from emotional 'ordinary-living' stress, are easier to muffle than obvious physical tiredness.

We keep them down with promises, 'Tomorrow I'll take the afternoon off, provided that ...' and then something else turns up and we keep on running. 'Imagine, I was only looking for twenty minutes! What's twenty minutes for myself in a whole day?' said Mary. Yet I remember reading somewhere that we make time for what we really want.

At the well ...
  How do I recognise when it is time to take a break?
  Would I feel 'justified' in doing so?
  What are my body's 'I'm tired' signals?
  Do I respond?
  What mainly keeps me on the road?
  Pray with this ...

If it is all right for Jesus to admit to being tired, then presumably we can too, but many people I've met say things like, 'I only really think about my body when it gets sick'.

Then they blame it, especially since they might have been introduced to Echinacea, or herbal teas, and didn't expect to be let down. But awareness of the body in the interests of wholeness is about balance.

I once worked with someone who had a very strong, people-caring, work-ethic. A quick gulp of scalding coffee – no milk – was sufficient for her tea break, and she rarely appeared for lunch. She ate that, heated-up, hours later. At night-time, she ran around 'getting things finished'. Always rushing, apparently without limits, and unable to say no. Prayer and reflection had long ago broken down. Things never did get finished, but she nearly did. Some months later, recovering and thoughtful, she said, 'I am never going to let anything do that to me again'. This comment made me examine my life too. What am I doing to myself and why? I think it was William Blake who said that we endure a profound hurt in serving systems, if we do not also attend to our own deep centre. Yes, of course we serve systems, but do we need to be slaves?

In less systems-oriented cultures, illness is described as being a body-initiative taken when we have failed to pick up more subtle

17

signals. If we are honest we do know when we are over-stretching ourselves. I find my shoulders beginning to burn and tingle from whatever I am 'carrying' and not putting down, or I can find myself with a particular swollen throat, which tells me I have kept something bottled-up and under pressure, for too long. Another person I know learns when it is time to stop, when she gets her 'good old reliable migraine'. And we all know the 'thank-goodness-I-can-stop-now' 'flu at the beginning of the holiday.

At the well …

> *When was the last time I was slowed down by getting 'sick'?*
> *What might my body have been trying to tell me?*
> *What systems am I presently serving?*
> *How is the stress-load?*
> *What am I doing to keep balanced?*
> *Pray with this …*

Does the body have to give such overt messages? If we are already tuned into its rhythms, probably not. We are then working *with* the body rather than apologising to it! If, for example, you are already aware that you are a lark, and acknowledge this, then you will be aiming to use your morning alert time for focused and creative activity, and leave the more routine things, as far as is practicable, to later on, and the absolute mundane, for the evening, when you are ready to stop. A taxi-driver I once met was very aware that he was a lark, not an owl. 'When we went to the Canaries with my daughter,' he said, 'I was in bed even before the grandchildren'. His wife was an owl, and her system operated the other way around. This was their experience, but the rest-wake cycle is rooted in scientific fact. Research into the molecular structure of what we call our inner clock (located behind our eyes), indicates that there are definite on-off times throughout the day and night, and that this is personal. This is good news if we feel guilty about getting tired when others are just revving up or vice versa.

But what is the point of knowing this? I suppose it is the difference between having a full tank and a clear road, or trying to drive with the hand-brake on. Do we honour the differences?

At the well …
My natural getting up time is …
Knowing this helps me …
My natural going to bed time is …
Knowing this helps me …
My creative, alert time is …
My routine-passive time is …
How do these reflect in my life?
Pray with this …

One of the 'off' times, apparently common to us all, whether owls or larks, is the post-mid-day 'dip'. So here is a specific time to sit down, just as we see in the passage above. But noon? When did I last think of noon as anything more than joined hands on a clock? Growing up in Africa, I remember at school, immediately after the Angelus bell, watching workers spontaneously stretch out onto the hot, dry grass in the circles of shade under the Msasa trees. Marking a period of rest. Years later I noticed noon marked again with a little gong for recollection, in a San Francisco Buddhist monastery, and in Wales, in a Carmelite community. And now, even if we don't personally ring an Angelus bell or stroke a Buddhist gong, we might find a way to become more aware of our connection with nature's rhythms, within and around us. And when we do hear nature's signals, what then? What can we do?

I think it comes down to two little words: 'possible' and 'choose'. We can only do what is possible, but it might help to look at what we do now, and ask, 'What is the smallest thing I can do differently, to make it possible to come a tiny bit nearer to what I'd really like to do?' For example, Elizabeth wanted more physical exercise, and she also wanted some quietness, since her job was busy. She was a morning person, and liked regular routines. She did some balancing of these particular factors, and wrote, 'I have followed my pattern of walking throughout the long, cold, and latterly very wet winter. It fulfilled its purpose, and was generally very enjoyable. This was because it induced a sense of physical well-being and gradually became a vehicle for a good part of my personal prayer. In the early mornings I know exactly how long it will take me to get to work from home, so paradoxically, I relax completely into my stride much better than if I were sitting.' (This extract, as with all direct quotes, is used with permission.)

At the well ...

> *If anything were possible, what would de-stress me, and slow me*
> *   down?*
> *Which might be possible?*
> *When and where?*
> *What could I choose this week?*
> *What particularly helps me to slow down for my own prayer*
> *   space?*
> *Pray with this ...*

When it comes to remembering to slow down myself, I have found the well-known 'blue-dot' routine very useful in my own bid for inner, rather than outer, pace. They are no more than tiny blue stickers, which remind me of the sky, and therefore remind me to breathe when I notice them on the 'busy' items around my house and office. The microwave, the phone, the clock, etc. Breeeathe. Come back to the centre. Of course we might stretch out and stress-out again, but taking the example of a mid-day pause, whether 12 o'clock, 1 o'clock, 2 o'clock, or blue-dot time, we have less to reel in at the end of the day. It does work, but we have to begin now. '… the great thing is here and now, this is the eternal moment, and if you do not realise it, you have missed the best part of your life …'[2] 'I live a half-day at a time,' says one wise old friend.

At the well …

> *What, if anything, would I want to change about my routines?*
> *What would I need to be doing / thinking differently to make any change possible?*
> *How would the change look in practice?*
> *What would I see as the benefits?*
> *When could I begin?*
> *What practices do / could I use to bring myself into sitting easily at the well, for reflection, and prayer?*
> *Pray with this …*

RELAX AND RECEIVE

Sitting and Breathing into Now

Read and follow twice as slowly as usual.

Seat yourself comfortably, with your feet flat on the floor, and your lower back supported or freely balanced. Become aware of the points of contact between your body and the chair and your feet and the floor. Relax your tummy muscles, and give a little releasing sigh. Slowly lift your shoulders and shoulder-blades upwards towards your ears, hold the stretch for a moment, and then gently release them. Become aware of the warmth of circulation around the nape of your neck. Now lightly place your hand at your navel point, and as you breathe in, feel your tummy swell outwards as it fills with air. Since many of us have grown up sucking our tummy inwards, this can feel slightly strange, even though expanding the belly is our natural breathing mechanism. Relax and just let it happen.

So breathing in through your nose for a count of four, pause for a moment and then breathe out (through your nose if that works easily, but otherwise through your mouth, letting the air hiss through your teeth as a sigh). Relax. Then, when you're ready, breathe in again for the count of four, hold that breath for four and, then release it all on a count of eight. Repeat the whole in-out sequence three or four more times – gently aware of your belly filling, then your rib-cage, then your upper chest, for the count of four, then the pause for four, as your system receives life-giving oxygen, then the exhalation, slowly on the count of eight. Keep it easy, your body knows how to breathe like a sleeping baby, and so no need to either over-breathe or hold your breath. Let it come and let it go. Rest in the present.

2
REAL NAME OR INNER VOICES?

Soon a Samaritan woman came to draw water and Jesus asked her for a drink. He was alone at the time as his disciples had gone into the village to buy some food. The woman was surprised that a Jew would ask a 'despised Samaritan' for anything – usually they wouldn't even speak to them – and she remarked about this to Jesus.

This is a love story but at this first meeting the woman feels antipathy as well as attraction. As she approaches the well, she has seen the seated figure, but she doesn't intend to get too close. From the detail of the stranger's clothing, she already has him summed up. Not for her. She will simply help herself to the usual supply of water and move off again. She knows exactly who the water is for, her partner, her children, and, oh yes, herself. She finds the taste of the water, like life, so bland, she had almost forgotten to include herself.

And then the stranger speaks. She doesn't expect him to have anything to say to her. His accent confirms what his clothes have already suggested. That's enough. She knows exactly what he thinks of her. And he dares to ask for a drink! Never mind that his request is relational, rather than an order and that it seems to acknowledge her presence; she doesn't choose to hear. She has her limits. Her relationships do not extend to include this new stranger. And yet? He *is* different. Obviously a boundary-breaker; like herself.

And what brings *us* to the well? How do we approach our place and space of prayer? Sometimes it is like going to a routine business meeting, or perhaps it is like going to the shop, or just asking for maintenance because our jar is emptying fast, and we hold it out for a 'fill-up' to keep us going another while, or perhaps it is like going into a nest and falling asleep. And which ever way we come, we come with some idea of how today's meeting will be, if only that it will be silent. Of course I exaggerate, but you know what I mean. Everything is fine as long as the One sitting there does stay quiet. But then as unexpectedly as in the story above, a word can break into a routine atmosphere, and the Jesus of our past, becomes the Stranger of our present. The dynamics change. Defences begin to surface.

Do we hear a request to 'let down our jar' in a different way? And if so? We might want to try, but suppose the jar breaks – we'd be there empty-handed. Anyway, this is just imagination, says our sensible self. It's better to withdraw from too much talk. We can still come to the well for some peace and quiet, and of course keep him in sight, but safely out of hearing range. Something along the lines of the retreatant who said, 'I have Jesus in the corner of my eye. I know he's there, but we don't get too involved.'

At the well …

> *How do I usually approach my times of prayer?*
> *What brings me to this well?*
> *What am I looking for?*
> *Do I find it?*
> *Who is there?*
> *What, if anything, has changed in the last six months?*
> *What seems to come up most often when I am at the well?*
> *Am I looking at this?*
> *Pray with this …*

The Samaritan woman doesn't withdraw, even though her routine and plan is interrupted. She is used to that. She is used to being a Samaritan, with all that means in terms of personal esteem and lack of self-worth. She is used to being this woman, hard-working, and largely unappreciated. She is used to being the water-carrier. Up to this moment she always gave what she could to those who asked, even when they let her down and left her to search again. But now she finds herself questioning. Why? What changed? Did she suddenly glimpse herself as he sees her? Did she suddenly glimpse him? Are her own resources suddenly insufficient? Does she wonder for the first time if her well holds enough for this request? Is it because it really *is* a request, 'would you? could you?' rather than a command, that she hears her own first choice? She is aware of something very unfamiliar. Here is a man, letting her alone to choose her response. Contrary to expectation, he has not insulted her, or forced himself upon her. She has the space to consider, without pressure, what her first real question is. It is about their relationship. We never find out when or if she finally responds to his request and need, because she has taken this chance to express a need of her own – to make sense of what is happening. What a relief when *we* realise things don't actually always have to 'make sense'. When we find the filters we've always looked through have been turned inside out, and yes, we're still there. But seeing differently.

Different Scripture commentaries have named the woman's response in different ways – astonished, puzzled, curious, defensive – and perhaps she is not any one of these but all of them and more, because she is basically in conflict. When someone sees us as we really are, I believe we somehow sense the truth of what they are seeing – positive or negative – and we react accordingly. Suddenly we become alerted to the narrowness of a too-tightly-held role, the falseness of a social mask, or the incompleteness of a never-questioned 'identity'. At the well, alone or with accompaniment, we begin to examine the origins of self-talk definitions of who and how we are, that keep us from wholly responding. 'Who'd ever listen to me? I'm just …' 'I'd never …' Yet deep down we know, although it can be hard to admit it at times, that we are unique, with our own voice, and our own strengths. We are loveable. Peter Van Breemen summed this up succinctly when he used to say, 'You're not loved because you're loveable; you're loveable because you are loved.' Can I believe that? Like the woman, what stops us hearing the affirming voice, 'you have something to give –'? And when we hear that, can we dare look in a mirror and say 'Yes, I am loveable, and I claim my own name and voice'.

Instead we hear our other voices – 'Don't bother with me, I'm cracked', 'I'm the one who just "did her best"', 'I was never as clever / pretty / popular as my sister', 'My brother was the one who went to college'. One of my own inner voices would have me always apologising (implicitly if not explicitly), for 'being so stupid'. This definition probably originated from a strict teacher in class who always threatened to put me back to class 0! For years her voice was the voice of God! A false god. My name was stupid. I had to sit a long time with the real God to hear a different name, 'I have called you by name, you are mine' (Isaiah 43:1).

What real name is the Samaritan woman suppressing in her reaction to Jesus. 'Surely you can't be asking *me*?' The implied tone is not from her whole self – we know there is more to her, but in this situation, another 'self' has popped-up, inhibiting a more genuine, spontaneous, generous response.

At the well ...
  What is my name?
  What negative phrases do I associate with my early years?
  What positive phrases do I associate with my early years?
  Which do I still carry in my head?
  Can I identify the original speaker?
  Can I bring reality to bear, and claim my own name?
  Pray with this ...

I once heard a speaker describe himself as an apartment block of which he was basically in charge, but which was threatened by a 'take-over' by various different tenants, from time to time. When

26

I mention this in workshops or retreats, participants often say that they can identify with this image, because they also have 'inner inhabitants' – between three and five, usually – who get under their skin as it were, and make it difficult to act naturally from their real self. We all recognise the more archetypal of these 'tenants' – the critic, the judge, the martyr, the child, etc. – and then we come up with our own – like Doormat, Busy-Bee, People-Pleaser, Plastic Smile, Grouch, etc. 'I looked at all of my "personalities" and they looked back at me,' someone said. I used to experience the take-over of one which always appeared in one particular type of setting, and rendered me speechless and invisible. However I only identified it and named it when someone challenged the falseness of it, by saying, 'Come on, don't just stand there like a waif!' Once I could experience what happened in my body and my thoughts when the waif was approaching, I could begin to re-claim my real identity, and understand that the waif's take-over wasn't necessary anymore. I didn't banish her altogether, since she had probably been trying to be helpful at some time in my history. So I accepted her being in a small back-room of the apartment, hopefully more integrated, but with no more take-over rights.

At the well …

> *How do I relate to the idea of an inner apartment?*
> *Would I recognise any tenants?*
> *Is any one particularly attention-seeking?*
> *What might it be looking for?*
> *Have I asked?*
> *Have I brought it to the well?*
> *Could I meet and befriend all of myself?*
> *Pray with this …*

Jesus sees the whole me.

If we keep coming to the well, we will see more too. To the

extent that we can connect with our real self, to that extent we find that the Stranger is not a Stranger, and that we are not 'peopled' by strangers either.

We begin to recognise the relationship within numinous moments; we discover it is not only we who make a first move, or we who only speak. A self I do not know, or may even not want to know, is being addressed. It is my call now. 'Our vocation is not simply to *be*,' writes Thomas Merton, 'but to work together with God in the creation of our own life, our own identity, our own destiny … we are even called to share with God the work of *creating* the truth of our identity … we do not know clearly beforehand what the result of this work will be. The secret of my full identity is hidden in him.'[3]

Real Presence evokes a response.

> *O Lord, you have examined my heart*
> *and know everything about me.*
> *You know when I sit or stand.*
> *When far away, you know my every thought.*
> *You chart the path ahead of me,*
> *and tell me where to stop and rest.*

PSALM 139: 1–3 (*TLB*)

SITTING MEDITATION

Find a suitable place to sit, where you can be undisturbed for about twenty minutes, and cherish the thought of time by the well. Allow yourself a couple of slow in-breaths and out-breaths, and arrive in body, mind and spirit.

Now become aware of the points of contact between your body and the chair, and your feet, flat on the floor.

Tighten up the muscles in your right leg, hold the tension, then release it and relax the leg, moving it if necessary, to a better position.

Do the same with the other leg, tightening the muscle, holding the tightness, and then release and relax it.

Sit deeply into the chair, with a straight, but softly-balanced spine.

Relax your tummy muscles.

Now bring your awareness to your shoulders, lifting them both together up towards your ears, holding the hunch and then releasing them. Repeat this, feel the shoulders drop lower than usual. Follow the relaxation down your right arm. Make a fist with your right hand, hold the tightness, and then relax your palm. Do the same with your left hand, make a fist, hold the tightness, and then relax your palm.

Come up to your head and neck.

Without over-stretching, gently turn your head to the right, then back to centre.

Then to the left, and, back to centre.

Finally, by parting your back teeth slightly, relax your jaw and cheek muscles.

Now become aware of your breathing.

Cool air breathed in, warm air breathed out.

In your imagination, let the landscape and well appear, and taking your time, become aware of who is there, and where you locate yourself.

You notice the figure sitting by the well.

What is your first response …?

Do you come closer, move back, stay where you are?

The request comes softly.

Is it one you recognise, or is this the first time you've heard it?

What does it imply for you?

… He is looking at you.

Who is it who is looking back at him?

Speak from wherever you are …

Stay with this –

O God, I am chained to my images –
  Daughter
    Sister
      Tomboy
        Brain
          Sweetheart
            Housewife
            Mother
              Chauffeur
              Cook
              Hostess

All of these am I? Torn?
  Disintegrated?
  Or none?
  No, I cannot deny them.
  They have become part of me.
  But somewhere,
Slipping silently between the images,

Is there someone else?
  Someone whole?
    Poet?
      Pastor?
        Mystic?
          Scholar?
            Music Maker?
            Counsellor?
          Lover?
           Friend?
How shall I know?

And you, God, are you also chained and hidden
By your images, your names, your roles?
  Creator
    Judge
      Father
        Redeemer
          King
            Saviour
              Christ
                Son of God
                  Holy Spirit
                    Light

Are you also lost among the images,
  Struggling to emerge into new roles,
  Fresh revelations of your real self?
Are you not also
  Poet?   *Becoming?*
    Artist?   *Suffering?*
      Mother?   *Loving?*
        Daughter?   *Changing?*
          Mystery?   *Singing?*
                  Rejoicing?
                  Darkness?
                  Despair?

Can we emerge together, you and I?
Can we break the chains that bind us
  and move out into the fresh air of liberation?

Call me into being, God!
And let me catch a glimpse of you as you really are
  in this moment of time and eternity!

BETSY PHILLIPS FISHER

3
BLESSINGS AND EXPECTATION

He replied, 'if you only knew what a wonderful gift God has for you, and who I am, you would ask me for some living water.'

Do you believe in blessings?

In Oakland, California, I met Virginia. She was a vibrant mid-life African-American, dressed in purple. She had given up a career as a television and stage singer, and was studying to become a Baptist minister. She invited me to Sunday worship. The temple was packed, and the service stirred with soul. At the end, I waited for Virginia to find me in the crowd, and when she did, her first words were not 'how did you like the singing?' or 'did you agree with the preacher?' but, eager, enthusiastic, *'did you receive a blessing?'* Of course, my first reaction was to look around to see if I had missed something external, a hands-on ritual perhaps, but then I realised she was simply asking out of her own expectation. She expected a blessing would be there, why not? Although this might not be the first thought that springs to your mind, just as it didn't to mine, expectation is the attitude that changes routine into response. The Samaritan woman is in routine-mode. She has walked this route so often. Her expectation is limited by the boundaries of the cistern-well, where the underground water seeps in, and settles. She is used to its quality. *It'll do, it's fine.* As she would be fine if someone asked her. But Jesus isn't asking her to only be 'fine'. He sees further into the more-ness of her. He recognises the passionate, alive woman underneath the 'despised Samaritan' identity. His request for water, as an appeal to her potential and her giftedness which he knows, now speaks directly to the hidden thirst, which *she* knows.

At the well ...

> *Do I expect blessings?*
> *Where have I ever felt 'blessed'?*
> *Am I always 'fine'?*
> *Is this true or false?*
> *Am I aware of any thirsts – longings?*
> *What would be a 'wonderful gift from God'?*
> *Pray with this ...*

With the mention of living water, new energies and therefore new possibilities open up, because it is about improved quality of life – inner and outer living. Traditionally, water, especially running water, referred to God's saving actions. Living water as Jesus uses it here, is a metaphor for the spirit and the gifts of the spirit that he will give. Whenever I ask a group of people on a retreat or at a workshop to say a word or two, about what they are looking for in their search for wholeness, most say 'deeper peace', 'inner stillness', or 'a sense of presence'. I always trust this will happen. The words of Jesus above are full of hope, even excitement. He does not seem to be setting up a reward scheme. He is offering a gift. Of course, we bring our own interpretation to his words as we read them – so like the woman, what do you hear? Is he wistful when he says, 'If you only knew'? Is he being playful or responding with challenging banter? Whichever, he is holding out the one thing the woman thinks he doesn't have. Ways and means to something she doesn't expect. But, just *ask* me, he is saying.

We may be very good at asking for others, taking time, putting our routines aside, but not always for ourselves. In fact, I find that when I pray for and with someone and use their own name in the prayer, they often feel quite moved. 'You know, I forget to pray for myself,' someone said, 'I only pray for other people or for things.' Yet there is no queue when it comes to asking in prayer. Perhaps, the thing that might make us reluctant to ask, is the possibility of disappointment. We ask in expectation, something different occurs, and we close down, or perhaps even protect our disappointment with cynicism. I once heard cynicism described as 'frozen despair' and of course that is a long way from a reframed vision or renewed hope. It is possible to be sustained by more 'in our face' values than by a reliance on inner listening and quality. I may not even feel I need more than I see, especially if my wells are all outside of myself. I can feel that life will be better anyway, once I have taken that course, gone on holiday, tried this diet, or bought that missing link.

It may also be hard to ask because those of us who are natural or professional 'Givers' can find it hard to fit into any other category. Even the gifts of God are for others!

And we may not recognise that we have any expectations until life and our bodies begin to tell us we have limits. 'Blessed are those who know their need of God,' says the first Beatitude.

At the well …
> *Where does 'I can manage' show most in my life?*
> *Do I ever by-pass real offers of help?*
> *Why? Why not?*
> *Pray with this …*

The Samaritan woman has been asked to do something she has done hundreds of times, and perhaps for the first time, she finds she can't. She can only offer a substitute. And he is offering her the key to get out of being stuck. 'Ask! Say it how it is!' Everyone has their own story about answered or seemingly unanswered prayer, but for the record, I remember a time, when I needed to specifically ask God something. But I didn't really ask because I didn't expect any help. It was my problem. Basically, I couldn't read or speak in public and as it wasn't about life or death I felt it was much too insignificant with which to 'bother' God. This was not something I had carried all my life; I had been quite flamboyant as a child. But gradually this had drained away, and even to think of reading aloud would start my heart thumping so strongly, I could actually see the beat. Of course this was panic, with the familiar shaking legs and squeaky voice, but knowing this didn't help. I invented some breathing techniques to get me through but knew that as I was a teacher at the time, and also involved in adult liturgy preparations, getting-through wasn't the answer. Then, after two years of this, in the grip of this inner paralysis, I made a thirty-day retreat in Wales. One afternoon, sitting on a hillside, overlooking the Clwyd Valley, I felt I had nothing to lose. I asked aloud for help, even healing. I don't remember the words but I do remember the accompanying experience. A strong visual image of an egg cracking open, and a small featherless bird crawling out of the broken shell. I remember sitting up straight and knowing quite clearly, 'I can read'. It took a day before I risked proving this, but it has never been a problem since. 'Oh, but where is God in that? That is just your experience,' you might say, and that is exactly it. We come to know God through our experience. 'If we cannot find a contact with God … in this very small world which I am, then the chances are very slight that even if I meet him face to face, that I would recognise him'.[4] My example, from that time and this distance, does seem small compared with other issues, and yet I remember it mainly because it was the first crack in my shell of false self-sufficiency. It forced me to test my image of God in a real way. And after that I couldn't push his promises aside. I began to dare to ask and expect – even with regard to physical healing – and have not been disappointed. It was at that time I began to consciously focus on living thank-you! Thanking remains a way of knowing. There is so much to thank for but we only know how to really thank when we know what it is like to lose. The gift of God surrounds us. 'Where are you, God, in this?' is the question we can bring to every circumstance.

At the well …

> *What do I ask for?*
> *I experience gratitude.*
> *For what in my life would I want to give thanks?*
> *My personal sense of myself at this time, qualities, discoveries,*
>   *recoveries, gifts,*
> *My family, especially in relation to …*
> *My relatives, especially …*
> *Friends, present …*
> *Friends, past …*
> *Pray with this …*

'Ask' is the word that Jesus urges and hopeful expectation is the attitude. 'What sustains us is our hope – and this experienced only in glimpses, in tantalising snatches of its embodiment in a short life-span – this is no reason why its language and aspirations cannot be outrageous. The transgressive Spirit urges that our hope be unquenchable as we plunge deeper into the mystery of life.'[5]

Gratitude and hopeful expectation is rooted in experience, and grounded in basics. Like the old man of the road I heard about, who would always hand back his empty cup with the words, 'God bless the dead'. When he was asked why he never said 'God bless the living,' he replied, 'sure just to be alive is a blessing'.

This is particularly poignant when our hold on life suddenly seems less certain. A friend of mine lost his brother to an early heart attack. He was talking about this with his sister. Not too long before, she had made a complete recovery from major surgery. 'Does that make your own life more fragile?' he asked her.

'No,' she said, 'I think I appreciate it all the more.'

I invite you to make yourself comfortable … becoming aware of the points of contact between your feet and the floor and your body and the chair.

Soles of your feet, thighs, sit-bone, lower back.

Lift and then release your shoulders, allowing them to become heavier but loose … and relax your tummy muscles on an out-breath.

Relax the muscles of your face, by parting your lips, and letting your lower jaw loosen and unclench.

Now feel the stretch throughout your face, from forehead to chin.

Turning awareness towards the present, and scanning your body.

You may be aware that your shoulders are a little high. Lift them higher, as if to touch your ears, and then gently let them down.

And again, then relax your tummy muscles.

Now bringing attention to your breath …

Cool air breathed in, warm air breathed out. Experience this coolness and warmth in your natural, not forced, breathing.

Keeping shoulders down and tummy relaxed, just listen to the outbreath, and let it be the breathing out.

… Starting with any person or any situation for which you spontaneously want to give thanks …

Bringing these into awareness,

Receiving them as gifts from God's hands.

Feeling them with you, whether past or present,

For as long as you need.

Then perhaps allow yourself to be open to receive insight about other areas of your life where you may not be as aware of gifts.

Stay with this, not forcing any feeling, just holding the reality as you experience it.

Now hear the words:

'If you only knew what a wonderful gift God has for you (name) and who I am, you (name) would ask me for some living water …'

And stay with that …

4
SURENESS AND CERTAINTIES

'But you don't have a rope or a bucket,' she said, 'and this is a very deep well. From where would you get this living water? And besides, are you greater than our ancestor Jacob? How can you offer better water than this which he and his sons and cattle enjoyed?'

A work colleague of mine was famous for saying, 'I don't mind being wrong, so long as no one else is sure!' I never knew if he had grasped something important, or whether he was just joking. Now I think he was ahead of the rest of us. Being wrong about something, allows for another try. Being sure, closes a door. We all know people who are so sure they know exactly what is best for us, they know the right way. Of course they don't ask; they tell. Someone I know had a friend visiting for a weekend, and at the end, she felt that everything she normally did, even the washing-up, had been critiqued and put right. She had been on the receiving end of this person's need for control. For sureness. The woman at the well has the same need. To put Jesus right. She is very sure, very logical, very experienced, very adult. It is so obvious. The well is deep. There is no question about that. A deep well needs a long rope, and a bucket. This person sitting here, no matter what he says, has neither, so there is no chance of water. There is no more to say. She is clear about the rope; rope has to be strong. Without a strong rope, she loses both bucket and water. Rope or logic is what holds things together. Sensibly. As I mentioned earlier, making sense can be our activating principle – and yet for some people this doesn't seem to apply. Ben and Vera, from India, sold up their home, to come and open a small shop in south-east London. This shop would sell religious books, medals, statues, etc. It would be an urban 'spiritual centre' with lunchtime prayer-sessions. But for whom? They had managed to rent what had to be the most unpromising venue ever, next to a civil-service department building, in the middle of a concrete island, surrounded by two fast lanes of traffic. Logical people in the know, myself included, cautioned them, saying that nothing would take-off there, because it was not near other shops or houses and besides, no one knew about this project. 'Don't you worry,' said Vera, 'Jesus, Mary and Joseph know.' Their centre was still running ten years later.

This approach wouldn't have worked for the Samaritan woman. Her logic is sensible and safe. Her trust is based on control but now, unsettlingly, a question mark enters the equation.

At the well …
   When have I ever trusted in faith?
   Where do I most like control?
   What might happen if I loosened it?
   How do I maintain control?
   What is the effect? On whom?
   Where, if at all, am I aware of control working against me?
   Pray with this …

With her use of the word 'but' the Samaritan woman reveals her ambivalence. As doubts creep in, she regroups her arguments and, as we tend to do, turns to personal challenge, making a case for all her assertions. This well that she visits daily, and thinks she knows so well, has been there for centuries, and is cut from solid rock. The provision of water can be traced back to her earliest ancestors (Gen. 12:6; Gen. 33:18–19; Gen. 48:22; Joshua 24:32). She reminds this Jew that her race also claims links with Jacob, via Ephraim and Manasseh (Joshua 8:30–35). Surely there is no rational reason to shift from such solidity and yet, as someone once said 'we don't need to build a prison for ourselves and sit in it.' And perhaps the woman does feel a bit imprisoned – her arguments sounding a little hollow, even to her, because Jesus is talking about water quality, not credentials.

I watched a well being dug. Once the surface soil was moved away, up came the stones – 'I can't.' 'This is not a good time.' 'Any other day.' After these stones, came the rocks, then the heavy mud, and finally the first free trickle. The trickle of growth comes when the tight grip of infancy loosens on the hard rocks of certainty. 'Certainties get fewer as I get older,' said a friend. So what happens then? Do we lose everything we thought we had? I believe what happens is like receiving an offer of new sight. Letting go means we hold our hands open rather than closed, and this is the basic attitude that grounds our gratitude, and expectation in trust. It is sight from the heart. Possessions are reframed into gifts '… none of these things are ours in such a way that they cannot be taken away from us, yet we *are* in possession of them. We are rich, and everything we possess is a gift and a sign of the love of God, and the love of (others). It is a continuous gift of Divine love; and as long as we possess nothing, love divine is manifested continually and fully.'[6]

We need to reflect on our patterns of gift – moments when we felt a presence that sustained or supported us, and therefore made it possible to carry on, even though we may have felt very small. A Scottish principal tells us the story of a five-year-old, who, because he was new to school, kept having to run to the bathroom. She met him on his way back to the classroom. He looked rather burdened with the weight of a life-time in school stretching ahead.

'Hello Miss.'

'Hello David,' she said looking down at him, kindly concerned. 'Is it *very* hard in primary two?'

'Yes Miss, very hard.' But then he brightened, 'But I love Mrs K.'

When we love the teacher, and know we are loved, we can dare to trust.

When you reflect on the fact that everything really is a gift, then there is a sense of adventure about the next step. This is not about being reckless; it is about being open to possibility. A wise man in Zambia used to say, 'When a child comes to the door of your hut and says, "Come and see, come and see", we must not say, "I have been through that door before".'

At the well …

> *What surenesses have changed recently in relation to myself, re-lationships, work, God?*
> *Where is loss in this?*
> *Where is growth in this?*
> *Pray with this …*

I believe we are able to walk out through that doorway and see what is new, when we are able to distinguish the difference between thinking and praying. Thinking stays with us, praying leads us on.

I used to regularly stay at a Carmelite monastery in Wales. During one visit, trying to work out my next life-move, I spoke with the Abbess, and what she finished up saying has stayed with me ever since. *'I know you think, but do you pray?'* I was shocked! I put in the right amount of time! I read the right books! Of course I prayed! Was I going to surrender my logic (or my pride)? In fact, I wasn't even thinking!

Like the Samaritan woman, we are invited to be sensitive to the boundaries of our thoughts and listen for the promises that take us beyond them.

There comes a point when we simply have to stop trying to do all the work ourselves, hold everything 'together'. Re-creation follows chaos, and spiritual reframes are often life's necessary paradoxes.

When we find ourselves saying things like 'It doesn't make sense to me, yet there's something "right" about it', we may need to do what the Samaritan woman is doing – keep the dialogue going and allow puzzlement and mental chaos a place at the well.

Of course, we can also put the lid on, right here – because although change is inevitable, 'growth is optional'.

At the well …
>   *If I think of the question, 'Do you think or do you pray?' what is*
>   *my spontaneous answer?*
>   *Is this how I want it?*
>   *Pray with this …*

HEARING ANEW …

Find a place where you can be undisturbed for twenty minutes or so, and sit comfortably, with your hands resting in your lap, your feet flat on the floor.

Lift your shoulders and let them drop back gently, and relax your tummy.

Become aware of your breathing – cool air breathed in, warm air breathed out.

Re-frame the words of Jesus into a positive, present-tense mantra phrase, e.g., 'God has a wonderful gift for me' or 'I am asking for living water' and quietly focus on the words, letting the meaning sink into your heart.

As you do so, you may inevitably find other thoughts surfacing – such as perhaps 'Am I doing this right?' 'How much longer?' 'This is boring', 'That was all right for then, not now' or 'This isn't real for me', etc.

Whatever comes up, positive or negative, just gently meet it by naming it for what it is – 'question', 'doubt', 'hope', etc.

Naming it frees it, and it can drift away, leaving you with the original phrase once more.

Rest in this …

DESERT PATHWAYS

I am a pilgrim,
Alone, yet not alone.
Journeying,
Always journeying along pathways
At a slow pace,
The pace of a sedated snail.
My journey of life-ing
Has many resting places,
Many cross-roads,
Many pathways,
Many watering places.
I pause now at this particular well
In the centre of Sychar or is it right here?
To sit,
To sit in silence,
To sit in stillness,
To allow
My parched soul to drink freely
Of that living water,
To quench the yearnings within,
To water the arid desert within,
To refresh my inner spirit.
I am a pilgrim,
Alone, yet not alone,
At this well,
At this cross-roads,

At this time of my life
I feel his touch,
I feel his presence,
I hear his gentle, reassuring voice.
Jesus wakes me at dawn with his words on my lips:
'Do not be afraid, for I have redeemed you,
I have called you by name, you are mine.'
I sit at the well throughout each day being held by Jesus.
We talk together.
We are silent together.
We are still together.
A sacred space.
Holy ground.

PATRICIA LENNON

5
LIVING VERSUS SURVIVAL

Jesus replied that people soon became thirsty again after drinking this water. 'But the water that I give them,' he said, 'becomes a perpetual spring within them, watering them forever with eternal life'.

'Watering' is a beautiful verb. Have we heard the earth drink? Think back to when you were a child, small enough to be really close to the earth. After rain, you could hear it sucking the moisture up. You can still hear it with neglected pot plants. You may also remember a film, made as far back as the 1950s, called *The Living Desert*. On a morning after the first desert rains, the camera leads us across what had been a parched wilderness the afternoon before. Now there is a huge carpet of colour – petals bursting open, bright pink, gold, chocolate-coloured rivulets swirling into crevasses and wild-life beginning to wake to life again. The commentary expresses wonder. Is this what we seek when we come to the well – to learn from gratitude how to wonder?

One of the most beautiful Old Testament stories on the theme of thirst, water and well, is found in the Book of Genesis, chapter 21, verses 14–19. In it, the slave-girl Hagar has been left to wander in the wilderness. A skin of water, strapped to her shoulders, has kept her alive so far. But now the water is finished, and she knows she can't survive any longer. And it is not just herself. She is holding her young child in her arms. Now she cries out, 'I don't want to watch my child die' and puts the child, symbolising all that is precious to her, under a bush. She moves some distance away, and weeps. Then suddenly she is hearing the voice of an Angel. 'What's wrong, Hagar? Do not be afraid.'

God has heard the cries. A spring is actually close by, and she goes to it, gathering her child up for a life-giving drink. You may find that you instinctively know what will be life-giving for you. You may also be aware of what it is your own inner child might need, if it is not to die. Is something precious in you left hidden under a bush?

At the well …
> *What am I carrying that is precious?*
> *What, if anything, is running out?*
> *What do I not want to watch die?*
> *What am I hiding under a bush?*
> *What is my cry?*
> *What would be my well?*
> *Pray with this …*

Living water is about life-quality, and it is about keeping it fresh. Living water is not stored, past-its-sell-by-date water. It is not hiding underground, just surviving. At one time, I was quite proud to use the word survival. 'I'm a survivor!' I used to say. But surviving is not living and, 'I set before you death or life', says the book of Deuteronomy, 'choose life'. The choice for life might begin when we experience our circumstance as wilderness, and like Hagar, find ourselves crying out, 'I don't want to die'. Survival is not dramatic. It is about just keeping going with a minimum sense of engagement, because you can't actually die. The Samaritan woman, with her recycled relationships trudges a repetitive round to an unsatisfying well.

What she carries inside her weighs her down. People have described desert survival in different ways – it is a feeling of incompleteness, a dryness, a confusion of values, but also, however hidden, nearly always a longing – *how I long to have a feeling of a greater presence.*

That longing is our sustenance, for longing keeps the heart guided, and the desert, the living desert, becomes a process. An experience of the liminality that is usually mentioned in relation to transition. Here, the usual parameters have disappeared; who

I am, where I am, and what is happening seems to be up in the air – there is only confusion and unknowing, identifiable in the experiences William Bridges describes so accurately as disengagement, disidentification and disorientation. Disengagement being a feeling of separateness from those places or people with whom we previously felt a connection. Disidentification meaning a sense of no longer knowing who we are. Disorientation, a wondering which direction to go next. This is a precious time. Bridges suggests stay; don't rush ahead when it feels like this, even though it is tempting to want to arrive somewhere, rather than endure this nowhere. As a spiritual director in London used to say, 'Wait, don't run ahead of the Holy Spirit.'

At the well …

When have I ever experienced a sense of disengagement?
When have I experienced disassociation?
When have I experienced disorientation?
With hindsight, what value was there in this liminal space?
How real are any of these experiences at the present time?
Pray with this …

Unless we have consciously withdrawn from a water-supply for reasons of our own, which is possible, but a different issue, we can expect that the desert will always be a process. The desert can then be beautiful. 'What makes the desert beautiful is that somewhere it hides a well.'[7] Psychologists tell us that, pathology excepted, there is always the call to life within each of us. I knew someone who often told me, 'I was so small I was kept in a shoe-box beside the fire but I survived!' Someone else said that at four pounds, she was like 'a little mouse!' Like Hagar, we want to live. We want to suck what we can from some form of nourishment. If our own voice is too weak at those times, I believe nourishment comes from the Psalms. In my own mind, I see psalms like 'one-size-fits-all' t-shirts – wide enough to fit everyone, because in the psalms the experiences are always larger than life. They polarise dryness, pain and grief beyond our own experience, so we can fit in somewhere down the line and find our own words met. Like Psalm 69 or 142. Equally we find our delight at any point up to the exuberance of psalms like Psalm 30, 100, or 145. In between we have the trusting psalms like 23, 91, or 139. But because when we are desert-thirsty, we don't just gulp down huge quantities, the psalms are best when sipped.

As the deer pants for water,
so I long for you, O God.
I thirst for God,
the living God.
Where can I find him
to come and stand before him?

PSALM 42:1–2 (*TLB*)

O God, my God! How I search for you!
How I thirst for you
in this parched and weary land
where there is no water.

PSALM 63:1 (*TLB*)

When, like Hagar, we are surviving in the desert, or waiting at the well in silence, it can be hard to believe there is truth in Jesus' words. How do we know that living water was even being given, and what does living instead of surviving even feel like? I believe we discover this personally, from specific shifts of energy which we feel and locate in our body. Just as a water-diviner feels the thrumming of the twig in the presence of yet unseen water, so we can find former dormant senses stirring in us. We 'sniff the air', so to speak, alert for the hints of freshness that indicate the new directional flow. The first shift comes when I locate where a trickle of interest stirs in me. Where do I feel this stirring? I am close to the Angel, ready to notice the well. With this comes the conviction that I want to change and grow. I may not like what I sense this might mean, but now at gut-level, I know I must go for it even in the head-heart conflict of 'But how can I?' For, of course, an identification of the well will have effects on others, as well as myself. But when it is the call to life, the means to follow through seem to appear. As invitation. As Merton puts it – 'Flare up like flame and make big shadows I can move in. Let everything happen to you: beauty and terror. Just keep going. No feeling is final. Don't let yourself lose me.'[8]

Let us focus our experience by letting this text locate our questions and energies:

So Abraham got up early the next morning, prepared food for the journey, and strapped a container of water to Hagar's shoulders, and sent her away with their son. She went out into the wilderness of Beersheba, wandering aimlessly. When the water was gone, she left the child beneath a bush, and went off and sat down a hundred yards or so away. 'I don't want to watch him die,' she said, and burst into tears, sobbing wildly. Then God answered the lad's cries, and the Angel of God called to Hagar from the sky, 'Hagar, what's wrong? Don't be afraid! For God has heard the lad's cries as he is lying there. Go and get the boy and comfort him, for I will make a great nation from his descendants'. Then God opened her eyes and she saw a well; so she re-filled the container ...

GEN. 21:14–19 (*TLB*)

At the well ...

> *What was 'strapped to my shoulders' in the last six months ... by whom and for what task ... or purpose ...?*
>
> *What is the most precious thing that I carry / value at this time about myself ... and ...?*
>
> *Where am I 'sent' ... is it valley? oasis? mountain? wilderness? How do I know?*

49

If I had to measure the level of my inner water-supply, how is it?
What is the lightest draw on it? What is the heaviest draw on it?
Am I stepping aside from anything at this time ... 'sitting down'
*   at a little distance?*
Is there anything that I am putting aside 'under a bush' –
*   something that is crying to be heard? What ... and how ...?*
Pray with this ...

We can finish this reflection pausing at a certain adjective, which Jesus used in his description of 'living water', as we began by pausing with a certain verb. The adjective is 'perpetual'. It is a word that we mostly hear in relation to negative things. 'Perpetual nuisance' or 'perpetual noise'. But here it is about being wildly lavish – not temporary or likely to run out. Our lives are very tied to temporality. We expect things to run out – our cupboards are always over-supplied and who doesn't store a spare or two of shampoo? – you know what I mean. But here, we are invited to relax. 'Blessed are those who trust in the Lord, whose trust is the Lord. They shall be like a tree planted by water, sending out its roots by the stream, it shall not fear when heat comes, and its leaves shall stay green: in the years of drought it is not anxious, and it does not cease to bear fruit' (Jer. 17:7).

At the well ...
*   I take time to ponder and pray with each of these words in turn:*
*   Surrender*
*   Co-operate*
*   Wait*
*   Trust.*
*   Pray with this ...*

Become aware of the points of contact between your body and the chair, and your feet and the floor.

Perhaps one or other foot wants to change position.

Shoulders are usually held high, so just in case, lift them higher, up to your ears, hold a moment, then gently let them down, feeling the relaxation in the stretch of your neck.

Gently move your head from side to side.

Don't over-stretch, just gently turn your head to the right, back to centre, to the left, back to centre.

Finally, relax your jaw, by opening the back teeth slightly, and become aware of your breathing.

Cool air breathed in, warm air breathed out.

Wait a moment and become aware of it, allowing it to flow, leading you into the stretch of desert.

You let the desert appear before you …

Whatever way this is expressed by your imagination you stay with this, aware of feelings that accompany this image.

You may be aware of words that accompany the feelings.

Note them.

They don't have to be full sentences –

Do they describe your sense of 'desert' or are they prayers, or inner 'voices'?

Stay with these a while …

Until now you sense the place where your imagination is forming an image of life – you become aware of colour, form, sound – a brief glimpse in the present landscape …

A movement stirs beside you and you become aware of the Angel, inviting you to approach, look and listen – your senses awaken you to what attracts in this image – and you find yourself talking about it to the Angel …

*'I know the plans I have for you,' says the Lord. 'They are plans for good
and not for evil, to give you a future and a hope. In those days when
you pray, I will listen. You will find me when you seek me, if you look
for me in earnest.'*

JER. 29:11–13 (TLB)

What brought me here? ...
  When did I arrive? ...

THE MIDDLE-TIME

Between the exhilaration of Beginning ...
  And the satisfaction of Concluding,
    Is the Middle-Time
      of Enduring ... Changing ... Trying ...
        Despairing ... Continuing ... Becoming.

Jesus Christ was the Human of God's Middle-Time
  Between Creation and ... Accomplishment.
Through him God said of Creation,
  'Without mistake'.
And of Accomplishment,
  'Without doubt'.

And we in our Middle-Times
  of Wondering and Waiting,

Hurrying and Hesitating,
  Regretting and Revising –
We who have begun many things …
  and seen but few completed –
We who are becoming more … and less –
Through the evidence of God's Middle-Time
  Have a stabilising hint
    That we are not mistakes,
    That we are irreplaceable,
    That our Being is of interest,
      and our Doing is of purpose,
    That our Being and our Doing
      are surrounded by Amen.

Jesus Christ is the Completer
  of unfinished people
  with unfinished work
  in unfinished times.

May he keep us from sinking, from ceasing,
  from wasting, from solidifying,
That we may be for him
  Experimenters, Enablers, Encouragers,
  and Associates in Accomplishment.

LONA FOWLER

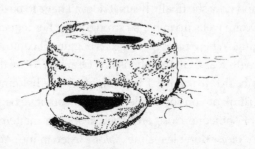

6
DISCERNMENT AND DESIRE

'Please, sir,' the woman said, 'give me some of that water! Then I'll never be thirsty again and won't have to make this long trip out here every day.'

I was once reading this part of the story of the Samaritan woman to a class of twelve-year-olds, when John put up his hand. 'Miss, does that mean never be thirsty for love?' He never knew how much he taught me that day. There was nothing I could answer. He had said it all. 'Some things can only be sensed, not explained', says a Chinese proverb.

We love because he first loved us said another John in 1 John 4:19. Love begins with knowledge, then response, and then personal engagement. We see the engagement in the way the woman has responded. She is relating to him differently, and they are there in relationship. His words about thirst and dryness, have exactly matched her own hidden, unspoken experience. Now she feels understood, so she dares to be vulnerable. She can at last use the real words, and the false language of 'shoulds' and 'oughts' drops away. For the first time she can admit even to herself what she finds hard, and admit that she so much wants for this to be different. She has done her best for so long, carried the water supply that was used up almost as soon as she got back, and now she finally hears it doesn't have to be that way for ever. Desire wells up in her so strongly that her request becomes a begging. When 'please,' is said as begging it comes up deeply. Often with tears. Of apprehension? Of relief? Tears that I might not be heard, tears that I just might. Overwhelming. Tears of hope. Think of your own 'please' when you have begged something of someone close and their response mattered – *'please* phone', *'please* don't leave me', *'please* listen to me'. You can't do it except from the heart. Give me that water! It is a whole out-breath of desire. A real want, not a just a velleity.

When I first met the word velleity, I had to look it up; I have never met anyone who used it, except the person who originally used it to me, but it is a good word and fitting here, since it refers to the *quality* of our choices. It relates to our level of desire. And in a velleity this isn't very strong. The dictionary describes it as volition in its lowest form, or, more colloquially; a half-hearted wish. How does that apply here?

Perhaps the Samaritan woman found herself talking to herself, as we do, as she trudged back and forth on this inward and outward journey, *'How much longer do I have to keep doing this?'* knowing that she is unlikely to change her habits.

But then, suddenly, that question, 'How much longer' – a very Biblical phrase, full of Messianic hope – is actually ans-wered. 'No longer!' Now is the acceptable time – *Carpe Diem* – Seize the day.

Yes! She hears the effect of this within herself. She is sud-denly centred enough to ask for something they both know is life-giving. *You know always in your heart that you need God more than everything. You need God in order to be.*[9] 'Please, sir, give me some of that water!'

At the well …
    What do I want?
    What do I need?
    What do I desire?
    Which can I let go as velleities?
    Of the remaining, circle the three most important …
    Prioritise and write a 'please' letter to the One at the well …
    Pray with this …

I wonder if you have found, as I have, that when you are making a case for something, you start to add all sorts of extraneous details, that with hindsight aren't going to be taken into account at all. The woman seems to be doing this, adding good reasons to validate her 'please' – it isn't yet enough to believe herself worth it – even if the trip wasn't a long one.

Is she just pressing her point? Different sites and places have been suggested as the location of Sychar, in the vicinity of modern Nablus. Was it As'kar, a half-mile from the well, or Shechem, over a mile? A mile to a mile-and-a-half in the hot sun, with a wooden bucket yoke pressing your shoulders, would feel long. If your heart was heavy, that would weigh you down further. Why did she come out to a cross-roads well, anyway? Was there no well in a village which is situated in an area with many underground springs? If we assume, as many do, that there was a village well, then the Samaritan woman obviously had her reasons for travelling outside the norm. Negative perceptions by villagers is usually given as the reason, but we can also wonder whether she was already acting out her unconscious desire for a different water? As we sometimes do, even while we act out, perhaps in an oblique way, our deepest desires even before we've named them.

How can we know authentic desire? Traditionally, this has been through a process called discernment; a way of attending to and recognising the energies that we experience as movement within us. We find discernment mentioned as a process as far back as the writings of the desert fathers (e.g., John Cassian) and the mystics (e.g., Catherine of Siena and John of the Cross), but for most people, the discernment process is known best within the Jesuit tradition, as what is traditionally called a 'directed retreat'. The retreat, a time apart, takes the form of eight, or sometimes thirty, silent days of prayer and reflection, with a daily one-to-one check-in. This is understood as the respectful accompaniment of an individual in a short period of their spiritual search, which of course is always about life-choices. The dynamic is based on the personal experiential process evolved by Ignatius of Loyola, as he prayed and listened through a period of decision-making in his own life. This listening was not only to God 'out there' but the movements of the spirit of God within himself and his feelings, or 'affects' as he called them. Later in his life, he was finally persuaded to put on paper what we now know as 'The Spiritual Exercises'. Very much a whole-person process, it has been described as an early form of holistic decision-making.[10] Ignatius suggested body-awareness, imaginative contemplation based on scripture, and both petitionary and contemplative prayer, as ways of finding how to respond to the call to life, to living water. The sensitivity of this discernment process means that it is about more than just focusing on an arbitrary, albeit intense, desire or want, and finding ways of achieving this. It is rather about asking the question of the desire: 'Where are you from? Where do you fit? Where is the Spirit in this?' What, in a situation in *your* life, are *you* currently discerning? What method of discernment do you use? Like the Samaritan woman we are face to face with an invitation from God, and our own deepest desire. We are also face-to-face with how we view what has traditionally been called the 'will of God' – a phrase which for many reasons does not sit well with some people, having acquired the connotation of a unilateral, pre-planned itinerary, probably going against the grain and definitely against nature. Spiritual directors and writers Dyckman and Carroll expand on this with an example of someone discerning whether or not to leave his ministry. 'If God's will is external to him,' they write, 'along with all that he has experienced, all he is feeling and hoping for the future, then this will is immutable and determined. His decision must be to remain where he is. However, if God's will is discovered deeply within himself as he reflects on the importance of choices he has made, his need to be faithful to relationships he has built up, his love of ministry, and his continued ability to feel and be alive and life-giving to others, he may be led to a new choice, with this new evidence, and a much clearer idea of what the deepest self in him really wants.'[11] This can be a dilemma. A term that seems to lighten the black and/or white of the above positions, is the one coined by Peter Hannon 'The Dream of God in us'. Emphasising the element of choice, but not minimising the initiatives of God, he writes, 'Our lives are directed by a dream God has built into us (but) the fulfilment of our dream is not automatic. We have to get in touch with it and decide to take responsibility for its realisation. It is very easy for this still, small voice of God, directing us unerringly, to be drowned out by other concerns. It is vital that we become more familiar with the voice of our dream and let our lives be guided by it.'[12] What is my sense of the 'will of God'? How do I relate to the concept of the 'Dream of God'?

In a directed retreat, passages of Scripture offer up their guidance to help us do this, as we listen to how our feelings and body respond. In ordinary life we can do the same, when our intention is to really co-operate and listen to what is being said within us. These can be the sort of body-spirit messages that meet us at a junction, and indicate more than a change of heart, sometimes even a change of route. Someone I knew seemed very stuck, marking time with trudging steps, like the Samaritan woman, but for no reason she could think of. Then she began to develop a rash. It was persistent and no medication seemed to help. One significant night when she woke up to consciousness – 'I am breaking out because I need *to* break out' – she made some shifts and the 'break-out' rash cleared up completely.

Right now we may have the question in our own heart – Where is God's dream in me? When was I last in touch with it? How does it express itself?

At the well …
Where do I hear 'the still small voice'?
What is my sense of personal call?
How am I facilitating the possibility of really listening?
What support do I have for this process?

Pray with this …

'Where your treasure is, there your heart will be also,' said Jesus (Matt. 6:21), and the essence of any discernment is listening from the heart. The Carmelite tradition of discernment asks that specific question, 'Where is your heart?' Sometimes we can tell by the content or direction of our day-dreams, or by finishing a sentence like 'I would feel my life unlived if I …' Or we may know exactly what our heart desires, like the Samaritan woman. It is right there, obvious.

More often though, a call to life as something more in the journey to wholeness starts with something 'cutting-out'. Like a tripped switch, our heart goes dead. We have lost our inner spirit. But not really. If we stay attentive, search around, we find it has re-located. And somewhere in our restless circling, the light is quietly burning. We need to follow its direction, for its energy is the dream's guidance.

At the well …
> *I outline on paper, in colour or in flow-chart form, my sense of God's dream in me, now and in five years' time …*
> *Pray with this …*

Because this is very intuitive work, with all the struggles that come in transition, it is helpful to evaluate our experience within a continuum bound by two words from St Ignatius' exercises. Doing this, gives a reference point from which to objectively critique an otherwise very personal experience. The two words, old-fashioned now, but understandable in context, are 'consolation' and 'desolation'. They are opposites, and in a time of searching in our lives, we need to be aware of them as a way of clarifying whether we are moving towards life – or away from it.

Unlike the Samaritan woman, we are not literally face-to-face with Jesus, and our choices may seem blurred. Instead of a choice for death and a choice for life, we find ourselves pulled at times between choices that both have life-points in their favour, and we vacillate between them. Here is where listening holistically helps and Ignatius is as clear on practical suggestions as anyone – If we are really stuck, he suggests we choose one option – probably the one our gut says we really do feel drawn to go for, rather than the one beginning 'but'. Then pray from that position and see what happens to your feelings, and your prayer, and your actions, over a period of time. Am I growing lighter, brighter, or heavier, darker? If you find you move between both, then ask 'Where do I tend to stay? And when I am there, what is my sense of myself, God and life?' Then you evaluate. Personal experience is personal, but there are recognisable characteristics of desolation. You feel closed-in on yourself, but closed off from others, and closed off from God. We feel restless, or disturbed by an inner darkness, and discomfort, even though we may try and distract ourselves from this, because we are arguing in this option's favour. Prayer is very cerebral, with a lot of back-forth thinking and arguments. Energy is trapped so there is a heaviness, and sometimes restless nights and disturbed dreams. By contrast, genuine consolation brings peace. This is deep-seated and remains steady even when the 'what-if?' sort of thinking comes up alongside. There is also a release of the previously held energy, and therefore a sense of relief bubbles up, and there is an outflow of exactly what Jesus is talking about. A sense of coming to life with the gifts Paul lists in Galatians 5:22–23. The alive person is joyful, can find patience, kindness, faithfulness, gentleness, and feels able to exercise balance as self-control. When these are authentic, the flow is easy, and easy to respond to.

At the well …

> *In my present prayer practice and after, am I aware of 'consolation'?*
> *Experienced as …?*

In my present prayer practice and afterwards, am I aware of
    'desolation'?
Experienced as …?
What discernment do I bring to bear on my experience?
With whom do I check it out?
Pray with this …

'Grace builds on nature. Is God calling me to live out of an en-
hancement of my known strengths? Or to discover the ones I am
only sensing now? – formative influences from without, meeting
responsive possibilities from within – and the word of growing
life is surrender, co-operate, wait and trust,' as Janet Erskine Stuart
once wrote.

AS A VESSEL AT THE WELL …

Become aware of the points of contact between your body and the chair,
and your feet and the floor. Sit your hips and buttocks into the chair,
keeping your back straight, but not tight. Relax your tummy muscles.
Now lift your shoulders and bring them up to your ears, holding for the
feeling of tightness, and then release them; repeat that a second time,
lifting and releasing. Then without straining, turn your head once to
the left, looking over your shoulder, and back to centre, and once to the
right, back to centre. Steady your head on your spine, and relax your
jaw, by opening your teeth slightly. Then relax your whole face, by a
brief tightening and release, opening your mouth as wide as you can,
tongue out, eyes open, and breathe out. With a sound, if appropriate.

Why not repeat this? Now relax again. Allow yourself to sink into your quietest space – become like the space within a vessel. From within that space, and as that vessel, you experience openness. Remaining in wide emptiness, you let your breath be the focus.

Then if it comes easily, you might attend to a sense of which gift(s) of the Spirit you feel connected with, and with a trusting heart, you dispose your heart to receive, whatever is the gift for you at this time. You allow your heart to respond to the words of Scripture ... making it personal ... receiving on a breath ... breathing in, allowing yourself to be filled.

'From his fullness we have all received, grace upon grace.'

JOHN 1:16

7
DROPPING THE FAÇADE

'Go and get your husband,' Jesus told her. 'But I'm not married,' the woman replied. 'All too true!' Jesus said, 'For you have had five husbands, and you aren't even married to the man you are living with now.'

A friend of mine broke off a seemingly promising relationship after a few weeks. 'We never talk about anything real,' she said. This is what Jesus is encouraging the woman to do. Talk about what's real. If she genuinely wants to receive what he is offering, share his life, then she needs to bring all of her life into this meeting at the well. A well was traditionally a place of betrothal, and whether the woman wants that level of commitment to realness, comes up for testing now. Has she spent these past years sharing her body but not her heart? Is she now being invited to understand that there is no real intimacy without truth? But there is no way this is going to be easy. By now, her inner secrets are all she has left for herself, and she is being asked to hand over even these!

When we are confronted with the same inevitability we may also do what the woman does. Jesus mentions the word 'husband', and she answers by pushing it aside and then closing her mouth. She is minimally responding but giving nothing away. Keeping her secrets secret. Most of us are good at pushing aside what may be awkward, but is still liveable, provided we don't give it much thought, and definitely do not bring it to prayer. Even when we take time out for quiet, it is still possible to bring enough extraneous material to ensure that we don't get too far into this aspect – whatever it is.

We know what we are doing and if we really do want peace, we have to, sooner or later, haul up this or that scoop of mud. Not as a focus, but a means. It is significant that Jesus has taken the shortest route home. It is more hilly, but leads home more quickly. Sometimes we also need to take the short route of truth and let what is, simply be there. My real body and my real feelings, however 'inappropriate'. At least this allows for real thoughts and real prayer. If we don't, and it doesn't, is it any wonder we'd rather stay silent, stay shallow, stay away, because who would want to spend time at the well, being unreal? How do we know if we are being real? Fr Carl Arico, New Jersey, answers this question in an article described 'Prayer as a Four-Step Dance'. It gives a practical commentary as to whether I am bringing my whole truth – at least in intention – when I approach the well.

'If I pray and read my prayers or get them in every day I believe I keep the Lord at arm's length. If I read and reflect in prayer then I believe I am allowing the Lord to change my mind. And if I read, and reflect and then respond, I believe I am allowing the Lord to change my heart. And if I read, reflect, respond and then rest, I believe I am allowing the Lord to change all of me.'[13]

At the well …
  What is my main 'topic' of prayer?
  What do I never bring to the well?
  If Jesus said 'Bring …' to me, what would he be talking about?
  Pray with this …

Having up to now only talked about living water, Jesus' sudden intervention about the missing husband is unexpected, but inevitable. The woman has opened her heart, said aloud what she really wants, and so he is able to follow on. If we say we want to go for life then his response must be the equivalent of 'So, what's stopping you?' An implicit question that only we ourselves can answer. Since deep down we know. Here, Jesus helps the woman out, by inviting along the missing husband. Perhaps we all have 'husbands' we don't bring along to the well – commitments, relationships, dependencies are left at home. Even while answering him, the woman knows she is playing with words. She is at the pivotal moment when she can stop fooling herself and others, and open up her story or remain separated from herself. It has been so wonderfully personal in this mid-day meeting, but she can't pretend this is her whole life. She also lives a shared life. I don't know about you, but sometimes I get a hunch about something I should follow-up in prayer and in life, like a nudge, and I let it go. I put it on the long-finger, and I suppose if I had television, I would use that as an avoidance as well, keeping sections of my life apart. But separation doesn't help wholeness. For some period of my own life, I lived with a foot in two camps, so to speak. My mind kept each sealed off from the other, so they never actually clashed externally. But this was not a whole or healthy way to live, and at some point, if we are basically trying to be sincere, we will be challenged by the words … 'No one can serve two masters' (Matt. 6:24). Sometimes, of course, we claim whole-heartedness and perhaps we almost believe our words, but actions speak more clearly.

At the well …

> *Am I aware of half-heartedness in any area of my life?*
> *Is there anything in this that I would want to begin to change?*
> *Who am I blocking out from my heart?*
> *Where am I holding back my love?*
> *What cultural, addictive or compulsive behaviours, have I also*
> *   repeated five times and more?*
> *Do I want wholeness?*
> *Can I bring all of my life to the well?*
> *Why not?*
> *Pray with this …*

Leaving aside any enquiry into the allegorical meaning of the five husbands, we might wonder here whether the husband or partner is mentioned because he was part of her life, and therefore couldn't be left out of a discussion on whole-heartedness. Is there a moral issue in this section? Many commentaries see a gentle reproach here on her state of life.

Whether this is implied by Jesus' words or not, what we do see, is an awareness of her that has the knowledge and the breadth of love, and which fills the gap in her non-reply. All along Jesus has respected the woman, and now he seems to leave it up to her as to with how much of herself she will trust him. The woman lives in a marriage-orientated culture. Once, twice marriage has not worked out. What was missing? Three times, four times, and she may have been wondering, 'What is the problem?' Then, who is the problem? The fifth time, and she must guess she is. And the sixth time, she doesn't even bother to pretend a marriage.

What did go wrong? What behaviour or attitude led to her, or her partners, missing the mark? I wonder whether what might have started as love, turned into possession; or what started as receiving turned into demanding, or what started as giving turned into manipulation. Is what we call 'sin' an overdoing of our gifts?

At the well …
Where am I with the following –?
Receiving forgiveness.
Recognising my need of forgiveness.
Desiring forgiveness.
Knowing what I want forgiven.
Wanting to accept forgiveness.
Forgiving myself.
Pray with this …

Myself as a jar … somehow aware of the clay, whole only if also in touch with the broken fragments …

What is presently blocking free flow into my jar?

If awareness seems blank here, then I slowly move my attention through my body, noting any area of tension or tightness. I place my hand lightly over or close to this area. I wait, staying with the sensation. Even the sensation of no sensation …

What feelings, if any, arise?

Is there any sense of holding something back that wants to come up?

What would it say if it could speak?

If words are there, I listen. Can I say them aloud?

They may not seem to make sense, but this is because they are the fragments.

Personal sin – resistance – resentment – falseness – deceit?

Re-makings is the potter's gift.

I gather my tawdry fragments – in the hands of the potter I can be made whole.

POTTER'S HANDS

'I hold you in the palms of my hands.' … God's words.

The God who formed us from clay … 'humus' 'human' … echoes of Ash Wednesday … 'We are but dust … or clay … or mud … '

But the God who gave us breath and life and spirit … and saw that it was good.

God moulding us from clay … strong hands … gentle fingers … a gentle strength … a strong gentleness … never forcing us beyond what we cannot take.

God's touch … and retouch … and counter-touch … God shaping this life of ours with purpose.

God once asked Jeremiah to go up to the potter's house. Jeremiah went, and noticed the potential of the lump of clay (spinning rapidly on the wheelhead) … all was possible.. and yet … the pot collapses!

So we too … we can collapse from a bereavement or from sickness … from a broken relationship or betrayed trust … or from a no longer tenable way of life.

'Cannot I do what the potter does?'

(It is God who speaks.) ' … as the clay is in the potter's hand … so are you in mine … '

The potter can use and re-use the clay … and so he starts over again using the self-same clay from the failed attempt.

This clay, already once touched and worked by God, is asked to start again … and becomes the pot that God intended … all the more beautiful for (from) the failure experienced …

DIARMUID KERRISK

If I try to hide in the darkness,
the night becomes light around me.
For even darkness cannot hide from God;
to you the night shines as bright as day.
Darkness and light are both alike to you.

You made all the delicate, inner parts of my body,
and knit them together in my mother's womb.
Thank you for making me so wonderfully complex!
It is amazing to think about.
Your workmanship is marvellous …

You were there while I was being formed in utter seclusion!
You saw me before I was born
and scheduled each day of my life before I began to breathe.
Every day was recorded in your Book!

How precious it is, Lord,
to realise that you are thinking about me constantly!

68

I cannot even count how many times a day
your thoughts turn towards me.
And when I wake in the morning,
you are still thinking of me!

Search me, O God,
and know my heart, test my thoughts.
Point out anything you find in me that makes you sad,
and lead me along the path of everlasting life.

PSALM 139:11–24 (TLB)

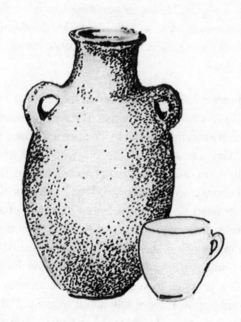

8
LETTING GOD BE GOD

'Sir,' the woman said, 'you must be a prophet! But tell me, why is it that you Jews insist that Jerusalem is the only place of worship, while we Samaritans claim it is here at Mount Gerazim where our ancestors worshipped?' Jesus replied, 'The time is coming when we will no longer be concerned about whether to worship God here or in Jerusalem. For it is not where we worship that counts, but how we worship. Is our worship spiritual and real? For God is Spirit and we must have his help to worship as we should. The Father wants this kind of worship from us. But you Samaritans know so little about him, worshipping blindly, while we Jews know all about him, for salvation comes to the world through the Jews.'

The words seem to flash in and out of the text like a quick sigh of relief. 'I see you are a prophet!' The sort of exhalation that indicates that everything is out in the open and guess what! He's still here! What a relief to find someone who hears what you say, intuits what you can't, and doesn't abandon you! The woman knows all about being abandoned. That is why she has learned to guard her heart. She has experienced a break so often, that she does not find new connections easy. And it gets harder. Yet what is happening now? Is she trying to keep this sudden contact going, by finding an appropriate topic? Does she think that if the Stranger is a prophet, then she should talk prophet language? Keep him happy, as it were; talk about worship. If that is what she is doing, so are we. 'I used to talk to God as if he were the Albert Hall,' said one English Benedictine. Or perhaps the Samaritan woman is genuinely interested in religious practice – a dormant aspect of her own life for so many years. Before this, could she raise any question about religion and expect a civil answer? After all, she is well aware that for religious people, her life-style makes her unclean. Ironic that it is a religious prophet with whom she feels safe enough to raise the topic. If her exclamation at the beginning of this paragraph is her guess of who he is, she is right. He *is* a prophet – 'one who sees'. Sees her, and accepts what he sees. One who has brought all aspects of her life out into the open for owning and reclaiming as it were, so she can move on, without excess baggage. And then again, precisely because this *is* the One who sees and accepts, the desire to worship wells up in her. A spark of spiritual intimacy. And then she almost snuffs-out the connection by moving outwards instead of inwards. She focuses on the details of place, because being a Samaritan, aware or not of the historical complexities which led to this anomaly, she has always accepted Mount Gerazim as the most sacred place on earth, not Jerusalem. And yet how could this prophet be so wrong about where to worship, and still so right about her?

At the well …

> *On what do I build my personal faith?*
> *Is there any place I cannot pray?*
> *What attitude and language have I prayed with, in the past?*
> *What attitude and language do I pray with now?*
> *Pray with this …*

And now for the first time since they've met, and just when she is becoming expansive, Jesus is almost dismissive. He barely addresses this Gerazim or Jerusalem question. How does she feel about this, I wonder, when her religious question is let go? But 'religion' means 'to bind' and to be bound by religious practice without a real spiritual focus is empty – 'just words I don't care about anymore' as someone said.

At the well …

> *Where is relationship and meaning in my experience of worship?*
> *What am I being invited to ask, explore, honour?*
> *Pray with this …*

But Jesus is actually holding the real focus. Relationship. In the woman's first introduction to spirituality, he is grounding their relationship in the essential.

He describes the Samaritans as 'worshipping blindly' – a reference to their syncretistic practices despite their ostensibly monotheistic belief (II Kings 17:40–41). It is only half a sentence, easily missed, but we might include it in our personal reflection around our faith charters, mission statements, personal value-systems, etc. Who or what is my God?

Jesus is introducing the woman to a God about whom we know only as much as we knew up to this last minute. For '…whatever we say of God is both true and untrue at the same time. God is always more,' says writer and *lectio divina* (a tradition of dialogue with a Scripture text, dating back to the fourth century) teacher Michel de Verteuil, following Thomas Aquinas. We know this. Just when we think we have our version of 'the prophet' understood, we are given a preview or taste of something more. I sense it especially in what I call 'care-details', and 'quirky-humour'. You may have found it by a particular sense of presence, or personal guidance, or perhaps by the inner application of the Ignatian principle 'God in all things', through beauty and positivity, to the final receptivity that allows in suffering and pain. This is the discovery of the world's transparency, where the dualistic separation between sacred and secular begins to fade, and a connection comes from the senses, as well as the heart and the mind. Thomas Merton described God as 'shining through' this transparent world, at all times. 'This is not just a fable or a nice story, it is true … We see it sometimes, and we see it maybe frequently; that God manifests himself everywhere, in everything – in people and in things and in nature and in events and so forth. So it becomes very obvious that he is everywhere. He is in everything, and we cannot be without him. You cannot be without God. It's impossible, it's just simply impossible. The only thing is that we don't see it. That again is what we are here for.'[14]

At the well …

> *How does this impact on my experience?*
>
> *How and where have I ever had a sense of God in all things? What happened?*
>
> *Have I sat at the well with 'the prophet' and experienced the more-ness of God?*
>
> *In what way do I know myself in the attitude of 'waiting on God'?*
>
> *Pray with this …*

From the first moment of meeting this prophet, the Samaritan woman's social constructs had begun to break down, and now her ideas about God are going the same way. 'This prophet is telling me about his Father, and using the word *"us"*?' We might pause for a moment and re-read the words of Jesus here, to grasp the enormity of inclusion that this means, as if we had never heard it before. Bilquis Sheikh, the Pakistani Muslim who became a Christian missionary, describes her own moment of experiencing the reality of it for the first time. She is in her room. 'I tried different ways of speaking to him. And then, as if something broke through for me I found myself trusting that he was indeed hearing me … Suddenly that room wasn't empty any more … I could sense his presence … Now I recognised this as the same loving presence I had met that fragrance-filled afternoon in my garden. The same presence I had sensed often as I read the Bible.'[15] The Samaritan woman is also aware of this presence, but not the meaning. Meanwhile she may pick up the energy in his voice, as if he knows what he is talking about. A Father, and more than a father, this God is dynamic, and finds us praying with recognition and discovery. I remember a time when I was living in a small, cold basement in Dublin, for some months, without a job because of a health incapacity, and no funds. I was aware of the importance of the phrase 'into your hands, Lord I commend my – not just Spirit – but *life*.' It mattered that I would be heard, because I was praying from a practical place. 'I need you as my guidance counsellor.' – 'Guide me towards the situation where I will get a job.' – 'I need you as my friend, because it is too small here to have many people in, and I can't get about.' – 'I need you as my comforter because I am scared about the future.' I found life became participation in – what? A life in the spirit? Who knows? All I can continue saying is 'into your hands …' Father, Mother, Spirit, Friend, Lover – You let me grow in your womb (Job 38:29); You love me as a Mother showing me moments of humour, and delightedness (Is 66:13); You hold me in your lap, when all I want to do is rest, and be quiet (Psalm 131); You are a Father who provides, especially when I am confused as to what I want or need, or where to look (Matt. 7: 7–11); You are there in my thirst, showing me sources and resources (John 6:7–38); You are there in my hunger. When the fridge no longer satisfies, and I need to look deeper (John 6:48); You support me when I dare to risk, with little signs that I am not alone in my out-reach (Ex. 19:4); You are my Guide, when so many inner and outer voices seem to be saying something different, and I need to listen to a voice of truth within (John 14:6); You are my God, because like Peter, I am saying … 'To whom shall we go?' (John 6:66).

At the well …

> *Who is my God?*
> *What particularly evokes a sense of the numinous in me?*
> *Do I seek and sense God's spirit in my personal spiritual practice?*
> *Do I seek and sense God's spirit in my liturgical worship?*
> *Where do I sense that aspects may be blocked or missing, if any?*
> *What questions am I asking?*
> *What questions is God asking?*
> *Pray with this …*

'The seat of faith … is not consciousness but spontaneous religious experience, which brings the individual's faith into immediate relation with God.'[16] We each have our own sense of this, and one particular spontaneous religious experience is captured in the inspiring little cameo from Bede Griffith's *The Golden String*, when the writer was in his last year of school, and walked out alone into the birdsong of a summer evening, when suddenly 'a lark rose … from the ground beside the tree where I was standing and poured out its song above my head, and then sank still singing to rest. Everything grew still as the sunset faded and the veil of dusk began to cover the earth. I remember now the feeling of awe which came over me. I felt inclined to kneel on the ground, as though I had been standing in the presence of an angel; and I hardly dared to look on the face of the sky, because it seemed as though it was but a veil before the face of God.'[17]

WORSHIP OF THE HEART

IN NATURE
When out in a rural environment, you might let scenery or weather help you decide which way to pray. Take time to let your senses receive colour, fragrance, odour, flavour, sensation, sound. Which is strongest, which calls for your attention?

What arises naturally in your heart? Does the weather speak to your mood?

Do any phrases of psalms or poetry come to mind? Will you move, or be still? Walking and praying, spontaneous free dance? Sitting and gazing in or at the wonder of Creation? Perhaps test which is for now.

What is leading me to praise / worship / gratitude?

If you feel drawn to the Creator, Mother, Father, Artist, by colour or form or intricacy in nature, perhaps when you are in slower mode, let this wash over you, as it were, amusing you, amazing you, delighting you, leaving your heart to find its own words of prayer, or none.

Or if you find some other aspect of nature calls for prayer-words from Scripture, you may have your own, or here are some that have been found to be helpful – a phrase or line at a time – Ephesians 3:16–20, Job 38:4–39:30, Psalm 8 read with your own name inserted, Psalm 84, Psalm 104, Psalm 108:1–3, Psalm 121, Psalm 139.

IN FORM OF LITURGICAL WORSHIP

Preparing your body

    How am I approaching a designated 'sacred space'?

    With what pace?

    Ahead of time?

    Just in time?

    Late?

    Is my body receptive or ...?

Preparing your mind

    What thoughts do I bring to this worship?

    Have I reflected, used lectio divina *perhaps, to familiarise myself with the Gospel text – opened its richness by giving it time?*

Preparing my heart
    What do I offer?
    For what do I ask?
    For what do I thank?
    For what do I praise?

DIVINE WHISPERINGS

Silence was so still
  I heard my heart beat
  as I lay in the sunlight on the sand.
Looking through lattice fingers,
  I watched one sheer-green blade of grass
Beating to the rhythm of a vagrant breeze.
In mystery, the separate rhythms matched.

EDITH GRISWOLD FAREY

9
You Have Touched my Heart

The woman said to him, 'Well, at least I know that the Messiah will come – the one they call Christ – and when he does, he will explain everything to us.' Then Jesus told her, 'I am the Messiah.'

I once heard a lovely story from a friend. She was telling me about her small niece and nephew, who were discussing God. The little girl was slightly older than the boy, and bothered because he insisted on calling God *Dear-God* – thinking this was God's name. 'You shouldn't say *Dear-God*,' his sister said, 'You're not writing a letter!' But in a way, the little boy was right. As we saw, and experience, God is relational, and perhaps it is God who writes to us. We receive through an attitude of attentiveness and a centred heart. Mindful.

This is something which has become increasingly talked about, and written about, but how do we find it in practice? Does mindfulness to the sacredness of now ever seem to elude us? If we look at the woman, we see it happening right now.

Jesus has been talking to the woman in the present tense – talking about now, and about a relationship with God in the now. But she takes the information into her head again, and uses it to propel her thoughts to future information. 'The Messiah *will come*.' 'We *will be* taught.' Facts will be given, and she will understand 'everything'. And everything will be clear and sorted at a future date.

At the well …

> *Do I live more in the 'now', or more in the 'when'?*
> *So how am I with mindfulness, and present-practice?*
> *Where is my usual focus?*
> *What ways do I have to return to inner attentiveness and the present?*

Her expectation is for the coming of not just *a* prophet, like this one, but *the* prophet, as found in Genesis, Exodus and Deuteronomy – who will be 'raised up' (Deut. 18:15) from the offspring of woman (Gen. 3:15), the seed of Abraham (Gen. 22:18). He is one who will be a true king and priest (Gen. 14:18–20). She already knows that the one who will send this prophet is a saving God, providing guidance and sustenance – Exodus 16:12–19, Exodus 20:1–3, Lev. 22:31–33, Numbers 10:33.

And she's mistaken. If she looks back to her own experience, she would not need to be told that she is already in the presence of the Messiah, and in a sacred space. Once when I was in this forward-drive, planning how life would be 'when', someone observed, 'but Anne, you are already living it'. Jesus is saying this to the Samaritan woman. Earlier prophets had spoken about the extent and quality of the Messiah's effect on living – 'I am sowing peace …' (cf. Zech. 6:12–13) 'everlasting righteousness will begin …' (Daniel 9:24–25ff) and the nature of this presence – 'The Spirit of God is upon me, because the Lord has anointed me to bring good news to the suffering and afflicted. He has sent me to comfort the broken-hearted, to announce liberty to captives and to open the eyes of the blind. He has sent me to tell those who mourn that the time of God's favour to them has come. To all who mourn … he will give: Beauty for ashes; Joy instead of mourning; Praise instead of heaviness …' (Isaiah 61:1–3). The woman has just experienced the personal setting-free, the provision of living water (Ezekiel 17:5–7), and the inner enlightening and enlivening, about which John wrote later (John 1:5, 7:37, 8:12, 12:46).

Reflection on these experiences would have made the Messiah's presence obvious. I remember an intelligent, forty-something academic saying to me, 'Oh, reflection on experience? Waste of time!' Yet wasn't it Socrates who said, 'The unexamined life is not worth living'? Why? Because we live experience in continuity. One of the dictionary definitions of experience is 'wisdom derived from the changes and trials of life'. Is this automatic? No, I believe it comes from prayerful reflection on what we inwardly recognise as significant, and find that we remember. Significant memories have been called 'memoir'. 'I like to describe wisdom as profound insight into life, living, loving, death and eternity'.[18] What is insight? Is it the sort of sudden 'thought' that burns into your consciousness, and seems never to be erased? I remember looking out of my upstairs window one evening and a sentence came to me so clearly – 'Everything is gift to the extent that you receive rather than demand the circumstances of your life'. It is something that has steadied me at times when I wanted to be frantic.

Sometimes insights come with dreams. Since this reflection is all about remembering, I will dare to share one more personal experience, although of course you have your own. But I remember clearly dreaming that I was crouching in a cage made of my own bones, which was being lowered into a hole in the ground. I was smiling, but had a small flaming torch in my hand, and was setting fire to my own brain. It was the first and last time I ever had a dream of such content and I naturally found it disturbing. But as I stayed with it on the understanding that dreams are always in the interest of wholeness, and are messages from within – 'angels footsteps' as someone once described them – I found a definite significance and truth about my present circumstances, which I was not, until then, able to consciously articulate. And you? What are your significant memories? Those moments or circumstances which brought you insight, indicated a path, shaped your present?

At the well …

> *If I had to summarise the most significant insight I was ever given, it would be …*

A significant memory from my childhood is … because …
It has brought me to …
A significant memory from my school-life is … because …
It has brought me to …
A significant memory from my teenage years is … because …
It has brought me to …
A significant memory from my early adult years is … because …
It has brought me to …
A significant memory from …
A significant dream for me was … because …
It brought me to …
Pray with this …

Memory enhances our present; when looking back, we see that we can keep on trusting. That whatever was out there, there was that stream or trickle of water that has flowed into now. I *am alive!* This is the richness of our inner treasure. The treasure of the mid-day years, when what is stored within, begins to provide more sustenance than what is without, eventually showing as wisdom's sanguinity and playfulness. 'All I have seen,' said someone, 'encourages me for what has not yet been.' And when despite this, some little unspoken anxiousness seeps in – 'What if I have to go and live …' 'What if I am no longer …' perhaps we need to interrupt the thought, and refocus on the source of our life and security '… you already have life and a body – and they are far more important than what to eat and wear. Look at the birds! They don't worry about what to eat – they don't need to sow or reap or store up food – for your heavenly father feeds them. And you are far more valuable to him than they are. Will all your worries add a single moment to your life?' (Matt. 6: 25–27).

At the well …

> *When I reflect on where I have been supported in the past, what prayer do I find for the present …?*
>
> *From the place of 'well at least I have …' what else might I include that I may not consider a gift at this time?*
>
> *If I look back on what I have received in my life so far, what is my response?*
>
> *I write a letter in reply to what I have received, and I say …*
>
> *Pray with this …*

VISUALISATION

Become aware of the points of contact between your body and the chair, and your feet and the floor.

> *Perhaps one or other foot wants to change position.*
>
> *Shoulders are usually held high, so just in case, lift them higher, up to your ears, hold a moment, then gently let them down, feeling the relaxation in the stretch of your neck.*
>
> *Gently move your head from side to side.*
>
> *Don't over-stretch, just gently turn your head to the right, back to centre, to the left, back to centre.*
>
> *Finally, relax your jaw, by opening the back teeth slightly, and become aware of your breathing.*
>
> *Cool air breathed in, warm air breathed out.*
>
> *Now bring to your inner vision, the memory of someone in whom you especially recognise(d) the presence of God.*
>
> *As this person becomes present with you, recall all you learned and received from them, towards your own wholeness.*
>
> *Allow gratitude to surface, and then, in your imagination, go with this person to the well, open to blessing – open to new truths …*
>
> *Stay with this …*

10
Free to Go

The hand will not reach what the heart does not yearn for.

Welsh Proverb

Just then his disciples arrived. They were surprised to find him talking to a woman, but none of them asked him why, or what they had been discussing.

Then the woman left her water-pot beside the well and went back to the village and told everyone, 'Come and meet a man who told me everything I ever did! Can this be the Messiah?' So the people came streaming from the village to see him.

Meanwhile, the disciples were urging Jesus to eat. 'No,' he said, 'I have some food you don't know about.'

'Who brought it to him?' the disciples asked each other. Then Jesus explained: 'My nourishment comes from doing the will of God who sent me, and from finishing his work.'

'It's very busy,' said someone about this last section of the story. 'Everyone is coming and going!' Yes they are, so does this mean that we are back where we started? Not really, the busy-ness here has a particular quality. Everyone is either coming from, or going towards, the centre. There is a focus. The One at the well. And also, presumably because of this contact, everyone seems to be behaving in a different way. We can start with the disciples. First they have actually gone into Sychar, and managed to buy, against all the conventions, Samaritan food. This has already stretched them, but now they return, and find Jesus has gone beyond them again. He is talking with, and obviously comfortable with, a woman. He knows, they know, and the woman knows, that the law expressly forbids any 'public converse' between a man and a woman. To do so, is breaking the law and inheriting hell. This held even if the woman were the man's wife. How much more here, where all the conventions of gender, race and status are being breached! Yet the disciples do not challenge Jesus. More importantly for our reflection, they do not interrupt this private one-to-one conversation. On the face of it, it would seem quite appropriate that they should. (They have intervened before – Matt. 15:23; Mark 10:13; Luke 9:49.) After all, they are coming with the awaited food and if they haven't already started eating *en route*, they are hungry, and assume he is too, since they will later 'urge him to eat'. We also 'urge the Lord' although it has been said that wisdom implies 'waiting on God'. And here the disciples wait. We also, in our ministering, whatever form that takes, learn to wait. We come bringing food and caring. And like the disciples, we also need to be sensitive to the moments when someone needs to receive directly from 'the rabbi', and respect the space, much as we might be tempted to rush in, rather than wait with sensitivity for the 'acceptable time'. I remember once wanting to be totally 'there' for someone as he worked through a personal grief. But he began to experience this as crowding. He also needed 'pain-alone-with-God' space. This woman is taking 'recovery-gratitude' space.

At the well …
> *In my caring roles, do I leave room for the Lord?*
> *What do I need space for?*
> *Pray with this …*

For so much! In the first reflection, she lacks initiative, she gets stuck before she can respond to a request, and she admits to finding the 'long walk' a burden. But here, she is full of initiative and spontaneity. Into the town and back, without being asked, and becoming the means whereby others' 'give me a drink' requests will get answered. And these 'others' are neighbours she usually avoided, so what happened?

Her needs have been met. William Glasser, founder of reality therapy, names our basic needs as belonging, empowerment, freedom and fun. Belonging means having a sense of connection or bonding; empowerment means having a sense of some positive control and creativity, freedom means the capacity to choose and be able and available for something, and fun is the capacity to relax and connect with an eager, playful part of ourselves, which is so important for inner and outer balance. The word 'relaxation' means to 'again loosen'. The woman is relaxed with Jesus now. Her actions show that she feels empowered, and the fact that she is no longer avoiding her neighbours shows she is free. She has also lost that cribbing edge to her voice and there is a lightness and enthusiasm, which is obviously infectious and effective. So now the villagers respond differently. The woman, up to now a professional failure in relationships, suddenly becomes inter-active. 'Come and see! Can this be?' Is she making fun here? *She knows!* They go with her. What strikes me most about all this, is that there is huge enthusiasm in her new spontaneity. The word 'enthusiasm' means to be inspired by God, and the woman has found her God. She has found herself home – a place where, as Janet Erskine Stuart once wrote, 'either the questions are already answered or it doesn't matter that they cannot be'.

She has been full of questions, so why is she peaceful now, leaving her water-jar quietly beside the well? Because she has bonded. The sense of abandonment which was so much part of her life, and which probably added voices to her inner apart-ment block, has been replaced by a sense of mattering to someone. Her self-worth has increased, and her former fears diminished. Fears? Well, truthfully, aren't we always a bit afraid when we so need to have the sort of certainty and sureness that she express-ed at the beginning? But now all that changes. Good bonding means that we feel safe and confident enough to move on, ex-plore and take positive risks. Bonding involves an exchange of energy, so in the context, her vivacity isn't surprising, and the energy she receives is love's. 1 Cor. 13:4–7 sums up the qualities of love as a gift, but in a particularly subtle way, mostly defining what love is not! Perhaps love cannot be described, only received and lived. The last lines express this quality in a positive action – 'If you love someone you will be loyal to him no matter what the cost. You will always believe in him, always expect the best of him, and always stand your ground in defending him' (1 Cor. 13:7). This is what the woman has experienced so her natural heart becomes the vessel, gifted and enhanced. She has become the real water-jar, beside the real well. Leaving her clay jar is a symbolic statement, 'I'll be back!' Of course! 'Abide in me, as I abide in you' (John 15:4).

The woman began with suspicion, blame (no bucket!) and criticism, but she finishes with love. As psychologist Virginia Satir once said, 'When we can blame and criticise in a real way, then we can love in a real way.'

At the well …
How have I met my belonging need?
How have I met my empowerment need?
How have I met my freedom need?
How have I met my fun need?
When and where do I play?
Pray with this …

Finally, Jesus is also acting differently. In other Gospel passages we have seen him walking, active in teaching and in healing ministry. And here he is still teaching and healing, but at a different pace. He remains at the well, and it is the woman who goes off in a ministry. She becomes the one whom the Orthodox Churches venerate as St Photini – the saint of light. Now filled with the spirit she reflects that light. And so we too can remain filled with light, effective out there to the extent that we are effective 'in here'. The mature balance of outreach and interiority.

And as we move beyond mid-day into the next phase of our day, we can check again on our own pace, sensing what is most appropriate for now, what is most true for us about this *kairos* time? We may remember that mid-day has had the meaning 'high-time' and reflection will help us hear this, like the woman, in different ways – 'it is finally high-time to …' 'It is really time to …' 'It is no longer time to …' For example, a friend, Maura, came to a decision to let a whole piece of her morning career go, when reflection brought her to say 'There was simply no more room for it, inside myself'. Another friend, Liz, signed the application-form for a sabbatical, and a new beginning. Like the woman, each was responding to an invitation to be her real self. And this is where this journey has been leading. Learning to live and love freely from that true self; or in the words of another woman, perhaps speaking for each of us, *'My mother always said I should be my best self; That that was the most beautiful person I could be.'*

Present to God.

   Present to yourself.
   Check where your thoughts are … where your feelings are …
   How is my body?

Prepare …

   Physically, geographically, to enter sacred space.

Remember 'Prayer is a Privilege.'   TUGWELL

Come …

   With expectation
   And ask yourself 'why'?
   Open to surprises
   Stay through boredom

Listen …
> *Another language*
> *Let God be God*
> *Relax … receive …*

Respond …
> *Words*
> *Tears*
> *Silence*
> *Posture*
> *Praise*

Oh Lord, you search me and you know me …   Psalm 139
and you say to me … (as I hear my own name)
You … are my work of art.   cf. Eph. 2:10
I will guide you … by a pillar of cloud during the daytime and by a
pillar of fire at night.   Exodus 14:21–22
I brought you … to myself, as though on eagle's wings.

   Exodus 19:4

My words fall upon you … like the gentle rain and dew, like showers
on the hillside.   Deut. 32:1–2
You … are worth more than many sparrows.   Luke 12:24
God fills you … with strength, and protects you wherever you go.

   Psalm 18:12

God is your helper …   Psalm 54:4
You are honoured … and I love you.   Isaiah 43:1–4
Even in old age … you will bear fruit, and be vital and green.

   Psalm 92:14

You … have been born anew to a living hope.   cf. 1 Peter 1:3
Your name … is written on the palm of my hand.   cf. Isaiah 49:16
Take care to live in me … and let me live in you.   John 15:4
I have told you all this … so that you will have peace of heart and mind.

   John 16:33

The Lord God will be your light … forever and ever.   <small>REV. 22:5</small>

Enter into the skin of the Samaritan woman – in imagination, walk with her to and from the well. Take different moments in the story as they visually come up, and ponder them for the day.

Take whole or part of one of the woman's sentences, e.g., 'Please give me some of that water' or 'You must be a prophet' and use it as you would a mantra.

As a form of centring prayer take just one or two of the words, and use them to still your mind, until you are deeply centred and still. As thoughts come up, gently reclaim the silence by repeating the words until you re-settle.

Find a picture of a well, a spring or a fountain, place it where you can easily see it from your bed, or from your desk or chair, and create the habit of gazing at it, without words. Let the image supply the meaning for you.

When did I last …?

  Sit by a natural spring
  Walk by a stream
  Paddle in the sea
  Put my face into water
  Swim
  Have aromatherapy massage, reflexology, etc.
  Dance barefoot in nature
  Reconnect with earth and grow vegetables
  Write my own psalm or poem
  Celebrate!

'You must live life in such a spirit that you make in every moment the best of possibilities.'

<small>JUNG</small>

A Gift

you have touched me
you have cradled me in your security
until I found my own
given me words
when they were unknown to me
tenderly you have held my heart in your hands
your firmness has given me strength
life itself wrapped in love
was your first gift to me
to love you is to love myself
to love myself is to love you

MARY ELEANORE RICE

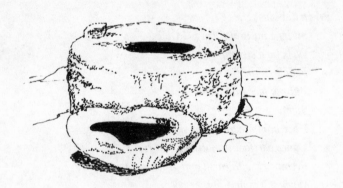

EPILOGUE

If you have walked this far with the Samaritan woman, you will know that the important thing was entering those spaces between the words, taking time, and letting your heart and mind fill.

If this were the last day of a retreat, we would be gathering any specific thoughts or insights that were particularly nourishing or significant. Some people might be thinking of finding themselves an *anam chara* to walk with them on their onward journey. Whatever it is, the purpose is to ground experience in reality and set up ways to keep the well open and the water fresh. The means are so familiar, we may have stopped hearing them, but if we have stopped doing them, then they bear repetition.

Review and re-designate your regular meeting time at the well, asking from your heart, 'what is possible for me?' 'What am I looking for?' 'What do I need?'

Then keep coming, no matter what the weather.

Invest in a timer, so you can rest at this noon without clock-watching.

Have two 'buckets'. One in daily use, to let down into the depths; the other filled with an 'emergency supply' for the times the lid sticks tight on the well. The supply is drawn from the same source, the lesser-known lines of a psalm, wisdom words from the sages and mystics, poems, journal notes, etc.

Expect to be surprised.

Be open to change.

Know you are loved.

I began this book by saying I liked the Samaritan woman. I am finishing by asking if she doesn't perhaps also like us too. I finished writing on a Sunday. And I placed the whole piece before God, and said to myself, with no way of knowing, 'Wouldn't it be nice if the Gospel at Mass today, were the Gospel of the Samaritan woman?' It was.

SHORT LINE BY LINE REFLECTION ON THE WHOLE TEXT ...

Jesus was tired from the long walk in the hot sun and sat wearily beside the well.

What in my life at the moment tires me?

What ways have I been addressing tiredness? What are my usual outlets?

Soon a Samaritan woman came to draw water and Jesus asked her for a drink.

What is being asked from me at the moment? Do I feel able, up to responding?

The woman was surprised that a Jew would ask a 'despised Samaritan' for anything – usually they wouldn't even speak to them – and she remarked about this to Jesus. He replied, 'if you only knew what a wonderful gift God has for you and who I am, you would ask me for some *living* water.'

What are my usual wells? When did I last ask for anything? What would be living water for me?

'But you don't have a rope or a bucket,' she said, 'and this is a very deep well. From where would you get this *living* water?'

Where do the majority of my doubts lie?

'And besides, are you greater than our ancestor Jacob? How

can you offer better water than this, which he and his sons and cattle enjoyed?'

What do I consider valuable? Why?

Jesus replied that people soon became thirsty again after drinking this water. 'But the water I give them,' he said, 'becomes a perpetual spring within them, watering them forever with eternal life.'

Has this been my experience in my prayer and spiritual life? Where?

'Please, sir,' the woman said, 'give me some of that water! Then I'll never be thirsty again, and won't have to make this long trip out here every day.'

'Go and get your husband,' Jesus told her.

What am I being asked to 'go and get'?

Sir,' the woman said, 'you must be a prophet. But tell me, why is it that you Jews insist that Jerusalem is the only place of worship, while we Samaritans claim it is here at Mount Gerazim, where our ancestors worshipped?'

Suppose she were avoiding. Do I avoid 'real questions'?

Jesus replied, 'The time is coming when we will no longer be concerned about whether to worship the Father here or in Jerusalem. For it is not *where* we worship that counts, but *how* we worship. Is our worship spiritual and real? For God is Spirit, and we must have his help to worship as we should. The Father wants this kind of worship from us. But you Samaritans know so little about him, worshipping blindly, while we Jews know all about him, for salvation comes to the world through the Jews.'

What forms of prayer are most real/helpful for my spiritual life?

The woman said, 'Well, at least I know that the Messiah will come – the one they call the Christ – and when he does, he will explain everything to us.'

Then Jesus told her, 'I am the Messiah'.

How would 'outsiders' recognise that I believe this? Do I?

Then the woman left her water-pot beside the well and went back to the village and told everyone, 'Come and meet a man who told me everything I ever did! Can this be the Messiah?' So the people came streaming from the village to see him.

Whom am I inviting? What do I want them to come and see?

NOTES

1 Bennett, Hal Zina & Saunders, Mike, MD, *The Well Body Book*, Random House, New York, 1973, p. 120.

2 Jung, C. W., cited in Wilmer, Harry A., MD, *Practical Jung*, Chiron Publications, Wilmette, Illinois, 1987, p. 3.

3 Bochen, Christine M. (ed.), *Thomas Merton: Essential Writings*, Orbis Books, New York, 2000, p. 56.

4 Bloom, Archbishop Anthony, *Beginning to Pray*, Paulist Press, New York, 1970, p. 19.

5 Grey, Mary C., *The Outrageous Pursuit of Hope*, Darton, Longman & Todd, London, 2000, p. 95.

6 Bloom, Archbishop Anthony, *Beginning to Pray*, Paulist Press, New York, 1970, p. 14–15.

7 De Saint-Exupery, Antoine, *The Little Prince*, London, Pan Piccolo, London, 1974.

8 Bochen, Christine M. (ed.), *Thomas Merton: Essential Writings*, Orbis Books, New York, 2000, p. 60–61.

9 Buber, Martin, *I and Thou*, Macmillan & Co, New York, 1965, p. 82.

10 Au, Wilkie, SJ, *By Way of the Heart: Towards a Holistic Christian Spirituality*, Chapman, London, 1990, p. 79.

11 Dyckman, Katherine Marie, SNJM & Carroll, Patrick L., SJ, *Inviting the Mystic, Supporting the Prophet*, Paulist Press, New York, 1981, p. 34.

12 Hannon, Peter, SJ, *Follow Your Dream*, Columba Press, Dublin, 1993, p. 7.

13 Arico, Carl J., 'Prayer as a Four-Step Dance', *Praying*, No. 67, July/Aug 1995, p. 41.

14 Merton, Thomas, extract from last talk as Novice Master, 1965, on the theme, 'Freedom from Care', from Bochen, Christine M. (ed.), *Thomas Merton: Essential Writings*, Orbis Books, New York, 2000, p. 70.

15 Sheikh, Bilquis, *I dared to call Him Father*, Kingsway Publications, Eastbourne, 1978, p. 42.

16 Jung, Carl, *The Undiscovered Self*, New American Library, New York, 1957, p. 100.

17 Griffiths, Bede, *The Golden String: An Autobiography*, William Collins, Sons & Co Ltd, Glasgow, 1979, p. 9.

18 Gilmour, Peter, *The Wisdom of Memoir: Reading and Writing Life's Sacred Texts,* Saint Mary's Press, Minnesota, 1997, p. 17.

Some Further Reading

Borysenko, Joan, Ph.D., *Minding the Body, Mending the Mind*, Bantam Books, New York, 1988.

Bridges, William, *Transitions: Making Sense of Life's Changes*, Nicholas Brealey Publishing Ltd., London, 1996.

Erskine Stuart, Janet, RSCJ, *Highways and By-ways of the Spiritual Life*, edited by Maud Monahan, RSCJ, Longmans, Green & Co. Ltd., 1936.

Glasser, William, MD, *Control Theory*, Harper & Row, New York, 1984.

Grana, Janice, *Images of Women in Transition*, Saint Mary's Press, Winona, 1991.

Guinan, Michael D., *To Be Human Before God: Insights from Biblical Spirituality*, The Liturgical Press, Minnesota, 1994.

Johnston, William, *Arise My Love*, Orbis Books, New York, 2000.

Kaisch, Ken, Ph.D., *Finding God: Handbook of Christian Meditation*, Paulist Press, New Jersey, 1994.

Keating, Thomas, *The Better Part: Stages of Contemplative Living*, Continuum Publishing Company, New York, 2000.

Rowan, John, *Discover your Subpersonalities*, Routledge, London, 1993.

Thurston, Bonnie, *To Everything a Season: A Spirituality of Time*, Crossroads Publishing Company, New York, 1999.